Trickster in the Land of Dreams

ZEESE PAPANIKOLAS

University of Nebraska Press, Lincoln and London

Letters from Raymond Taylor
reprinted with permission of
Samuel W. Taylor and of the
Special Collections at the
Marriott Library, University of
Utah. © 1995 by the University of
Nebraska Press. All rights reserved.
Manufactured in the United
States of America. ⊛ The paper in
this book meets the minimum
requirements of American National
Standard for Information Sciences —
Permanence of Paper for Printed
Library Materials, ANSI Z39.48-1984.
Library of Congress Cataloging-
in-Publication Data. Papanikolas,
Zeese. Trickster in the land of
dreams / Zeese Papanikolas. p. cm.
Includes index.
ISBN 0-8032-3703-0 (alk. paper)
1. Shoshoni mythology. 2. Trickster —
West (U.S.) 3. Technological inno-
vations — West (U.S.) 4. Utopias —
West (U.S.) 5. West (U.S.) — History.
6. West (U.S.) — Social life and customs.
I. Title. E99.S4P36   1995
398'.0978 — dc20   94-36924   CIP

For my mother and father

My first interpreters of the American West

Contents

This book is a study of the themes of technological innovation and utopianism that have been embedded in the mythologies of the American West from the Stone Age to the present day. There are some subthemes running through most of these chapters. Gambling is one of them, and illusion, and the primeval theme of the Quest. And dancing through all of these pages is the figure of the Trickster, from his Native American embodiment as Coyote, to P. T. Barnum and the Wizard of Oz.

Readers familiar with the work of Paul Radin and Claude Lévi-Strauss will have no difficulty in finding their influence in my re-creations of Shoshonean mythology, and in other places in this book the influence of Leo Marx and Henry Nash Smith will be evident. And my view of Mark Twain as Bad Boy owes much to Dwight Macdonald's treatment of him in *Against the American Grain* (1962). I wrote the second chapter of this book, a brief account of some of the animating motives behind the Spaniards' quest for the cities of Cíbola, before I had read Stephen Greenblatt's fine study of the European encounter with the Americas *Marvelous Possessions: The Wonder of the New World* (1991). Greenblatt explores with much subtlety the themes of language and appropriation in the first centuries of European contact with the New World that my chapter treats briefly and, in the case of Montaigne especially, with different emphasis. Readers interested in a scholar's approach to these topics should certainly read him. I am also indebted to Stuart Culver's treatment of the psychology and economics of the Land of Oz in his essay "What Manikins Want: *the Wonderful Wizard of Oz* and *The Art of Decorating Dry Goods Windows*," *Representations* 21 (Winter 1988).

I owe debts to many people who helped me in large ways and small in the writing of this book, but especially to Frank Bergon, who read carefully but bears no responsibility for the mistakes and grotesqueries in this volume, and to my wife Ruth Fallenbaum, who heard (and kept on hearing) most of the thoughts on these pages long before she read them.

Trickster in the Land of Dreams

O Stop and tell me, Red Man, who are you, why you roam,
And how you get your living; have you no God, no home?

Mormon hymn

Dust People

I   SHADOWS

In a world without fire, on a plain, the creatures of the mythtime are gathered. They have come together for a handgame, or to hunt rabbits. Coyote is there, and Lizard, and Hummingbird with his pretty feathers. But the world in which they gather is a cold place. A lightless place. Back and forth the creatures go on the lightless, limitless plane, chafing themselves, shadows of who they will one day be. We do not know what real fire is, Coyote says. We haven't been using real fire.

Because a world without fire, like a world without desire, cannot exist. It cannot be conscious of itself. For fire is a kind of speech, a tongue. It is impossible to imagine a story without imagining a fire.

An ash floats down. Coyote sees it, cocks his head. Ash is the ghost of fire, the evidence of its absence. Coyote cocks his head at the ash and invents desire.

Two worlds are now possible, where only the boundaryless, unshaped world of unconsciousness was before. The world of fire is the world that must be created so that our world can imagine itself.

The birds fly up: Coyote sends them. Eagle falls back. So does Hawk. Finally Hummingbird flies up. He keeps going and he sees the fires smoking far in the West. The yonder has been made.

So the creatures of the mythtime set out across the Dusty Path to bring back fire. The way will be waterless and full of tricks. And the road between the

I

two worlds is the road of desire. But to say desire is in the world is the same as saying that the story will not end until its object has been reached.

2 BEGINNINGS

The primitive stages can always be reestablished;
the primitive mind is, in the fullest meaning of the word,
imperishable. Sigmund Freud

Toward noon on those long summer days things wobble and shimmer with heat and the color is bled out of the landscape. The long ranges of mountains rise up from the dry valleys in waves: bone, bleached, monotonous. It is a hard land to judge at that hour. A peak that seems so near that it might be an hour's walk hangs in the air, never getting closer, never changing. Then the sun begins to drop. Strange shadows elongate themselves from the skirts of the mountains, peaks float over pools of blue shade, whirl-winds ride spookily across the empty spaces.

For more than 7,000 years it has been dry here. The summer thunder-showers leave little trace an hour after they have gone, and the journeys between the few springs and fewer streams and desert lakes are long and pitiless for travelers afoot. The heat, the aridity, affect the way things sit in the mind. A desert traveler once watched a coyote trot through a water-mirage in a dry basin. In the shimmering heat the coyote was transformed into a wolf swimming across a lake. "The reality is one thing," the traveler wrote, "the appearance quite another thing; but why are not both of them truthful?"

An hour or two before dusk, the far mountains begin to emerge from the gray wash of light. Deep cracks and striations appear in their faces, the individual stages of the rubble skirts emerge from the distance; the colors become differentiated into blues, pinks, greens. Gradually night comes. The stars are incredible. The Milky Way is a wipe of silver in the clear, black sky. For the People, the native inhabitants of this desert, it was the road to the other world, the land of the dead. They called it the Dusty Path, and sent their shamans along it to bring back souls who had gotten lost, as Coyote and his fellow creatures once followed it to bring back the secret of fire when the earth was new. The People knew as well as anyone that reality was a form of consent. The world resides within as much as without.

..

The tales at first seem strange. They should seem strange. Odd things happen. Animals slip into the skins of human beings and humans become animals. Two brothers turn into mourning doves, alight at a water hole at dawn, puff out their chests, drink, and are men again. An antelope with a thousand eyes guards an ogre. Cottontail shoots down the sun. Coyote's penis detaches itself, goes off on adventures of its own. A hero is born out of a clot of blood. It is a world of man-eating suns, of giants and talking excrements, of women with teeth between their legs and of a race of cannibals who have no anuses. In the winter, when the snakes were in their dens and the stories could be told, the People sat around the cooking fires or huddled under the rabbitskin blankets and told of the first things. In that moment of telling the mythtime was really there, Elder Brother Wolf with his schemes of utopia, Coyote with his cocked head and terminal stutter, rose up in the smoke, and the world was still being formed. Like some many-dimensional patchwork quilt that existed only in the mind, every story was a part of every other story. When white people first came to record these tales in books and, later, with sound devices, what came to be preserved was only a pale transcript, a fragment. For story was a texture, a space, a performance that was always happening, never complete. It did not go off like an arrow straight to some preordained target, but was an interval that summoned up the other intervals of the People's being. For the lives of such letterless folk are their poetry: ritual, costume, the way they cook or hunt — the symmetries and asymmetries, metaphors, and contiguities of their daily reality — all these are meanings that cannot be teased out of their living tissue, meanings that can only be in some manner falsified if they are defined. We, who have so burdened the world with our Sphinxes and our billboards, our Louvres and our Parthenons, have difficulty understanding a race whose art was stored in memory alone, who traveled light. Our great literary achievement, the nineteenth-century novel, aspired to an aesthetic of wholeness because the culture it came out of was already breaking up. The People's culture was intact. One needed only speak a part to summon up the whole.

And there never was a falling away. In all of the tales, there never was a longed-for Golden Age, no Angel's sword blocking the road back to Eden, no mythical past reflected only in the shards and ruins of an impoverished present. If the mythtime began with Wolf's Utopia, it didn't end there. There was no nostalgia and there was no tragedy. The world the People had was the world they desired. And so they embarked on that most difficult of speculations: imagining how it might have been otherwise. How it might have been before Cottontail or Wolf or Coyote gave the world its present form. And above all, they imagined in that most daring of all leaps, a world before humankind. For to think of a world without people is a way of asking who people are, what connects and what divides them from the rest of nature. It is thinking done in things, and in the way they are discovered, and in the lines of their resemblances. For all its gratuitous bloodshed, its trickiness, its bizarre sexuality, its sadism, the People's imaginary world was finally a less harsh and more realistic place than our own. Its mixture of cruelty and pleasure had not been partitioned into a rationalized scheme of Heaven and Hell, nor had it faced the technician's empty future. It was a world heavy in shame and mockery, but remarkably lacking in guilt, and it was a world without ideas. For in these tales it is laughter that takes the place of idea. Laughter, that in its anarchy swallows the categories of evil and good, confounds them in experience and creates a world that is neither the one nor the other, but a mixture of both, and human beings who remembering that, remember also whose progeny they are, listening to Coyote's brittle, mocking bark in the silence of the desert. So, in their first stories, the People created themselves. It may have been this way, they said.

The Temptation

We are in some strange country now. There is no yonder in this country. There is no future and there is no past. There is only Coyote, cocking his head, bemused to find himself stranded in this primitive landscape. Everything that exists shines with a sort of glow, as if there were only one object like it in the world. The hut, the line of willows along the little creek – there is no border that separates Coyote from what he sees, no exterior world distinct from Coyote's inner one. In fact, there is no inside at all here. The inside hasn't been invented yet. That is up to the future, but the future hasn't been invented yet either. Coyote sits in the shade of the wickiup with his legs straight out in front of him like a savage, mending a rabbit net, waiting for Elder Brother Wolf to come home.

Away over yonder, in some watery land to the west, unknown to Coyote and Wolf, there live two women. Primeval, eternal, remnants of that ancient time when earth was made bit by bit out of handfuls of mud drawn up from the endless sea.

Maybe the two of them had always existed. Who knows? You couldn't imagine them being fathered. They seemed to have just happened. Maybe

4

they weren't born at all. Maybe they just hatched, like the ducks and swans that swam and honked and clucked all around them, or the geese flying in long Vs overhead. Men like to think of every woman as a little story. An anecdote. These women were beyond fiction – or prior to it. They didn't dig for roots, like the women to come, nor did they gather or fish, for fish were trapped in weirs or baskets, harvested like seeds. They hunted the web-footed birds that flocked to their island and flapped their wings between water and sky. Laughing and clucking to each other, hunting, telling jokes, pissing in the weeds, Water Girl and her mother weren't stories at all. They just were. These women had no art. They had no wiles, no double meanings. They had only one secret.

Two worlds, separate, self-sufficient, self-contained. That watery world of the Amazon huntresses, the masculine world of Coyote and Wolf, with its easy life of the camp and the chase, its whiff of homoerotic camaraderie. Innocent, knowledgeless, ready to end. One day (has she reached puberty?) the girl is sent out to find a man.

Coyote is sitting in front of the wickiup mending the rabbit net. He doesn't know such things as women exist. Then the girl appears. She asks for Wolf. Coyote looks at her. A yellow light glows strangely from her skin. The white puff of a rabbit's tail twitches suggestively above her plump buttocks. Coyote says that Wolf is dead.

The girl flies over the sagebrush and it vibrates with her passing. Coyote follows after, always teased forward, farther and farther from the land of Brother Wolf. From camp to camp she leads him on. Who's the quarry, after all? Chasing her off into the bush, Coyote trips over his own rabbit net. Lust is turning the tables on Coyote. It always will.

The border between one world and the next, between life and death, between the world of women and the world of men, cannot be negotiated by ordinary means. They come to the edge of the lake the river the sea that separates Water Girl from her island home (in a Paiute tale she squats to urinate, it becomes a lake); she flies across the water and Coyote is left stranded.

Now he's helpless. The girl herself must carry him across the water to her home. In his eagerness, Coyote attempts to take advantage of her in mid-stream. She dumps him into the water, but Coyote, who, if he is a fool is still a wizard, turns himself into a waterskate and makes the crossing. Finally he is on the other side. He decks himself out like a young buck to go courting, with fringed leggings and beads, an ornament through his nose.

He puts a bit of abalone shell into his mouth. The shell glows green and uncanny when he grins. He preens. He thinks he's rather handsome.

Vain, ingenious, filled with all the cleverness of a hero and cowardly as a snake, Coyote stands there, with one paw in our own time and the other in the world of myth. He is Trickster, a mountebank, a wizard *manqué*. Half god, half idiot, he is the primal dandy, the culture maker. It isn't up to Wolf, the hunter, the dour inventor of utopias inhuman in their perfection to make our life. It is Coyote, the scavenger, the carrion eater, who makes the world of human beings. He smashes Wolf's sterile utopias to smithereens and remakes the world out of his mistakes. He lets the animals out of Wolf's cave and they scatter: henceforth hunting will be difficult. He begs and the seasons are divided: now winter will be long. He whines so loudly that death comes into the world. Trickster, dupe, failure, who cannot contain himself, who shits himself always, earthy, brilliant, excremental, would-be fucker of his own daughters – it is Coyote who will be our father.

Coyote stands on the margins of the world of women, adorned like a suitor, peering into the darkness of the wickiup.

The Wickiup

It lookes like an inverted basket, or like a water bottle, or like the caps the women weave for themselves, a frame of willows shingled with cedar bark. Coyote, as will his children ever after, squats down and squeezes through the narrow door. Womb, home, and, as we will soon see, potential tomb, the beginning of the human race starts out with our father crawling head-first into the world of women on all fours.

In the dark interior there is only the old woman. The girl is out hunting. Coyote curls up to wait. He notices in the dim light that the walls of the wickiup are hung with quivers and bows. What good times there will be when all these men return! Coyote thinks. He doesn't stop to ask why they have left without their weapons. And if so, where they have gone.

Now Water Girl comes home from the hunt, strung from her waist the water birds who are her prey, duck and swan and goose. Coyote is an honored guest. The women pluck the birds and throw them into the pot. Coyote's abalone shell shines greenly in the darkness as he smirks.

On his good behavior for the time being, a suitor, Coyote eats daintily (he will gorge himself after everyone else is asleep). Coyote is at his ease. He watches the women dip their fingers into the meat pot and eat, enjoys the sound of their smacking lips and the grease glowing on their chins. But when the women have cleaned the meat, without more ado they put the bones under their skirts. And then Coyote hears something that turns him yellow with fear: from under their skirts comes the sound of the cracking of bones and the gnashing of teeth!

Is it the territory of Freud we've entered? Or, more primitively, is this the lurid mental landscape of his wilder followers, where the infantile urges of the sucking child engender primal terrors, and the devourer becomes the devoured? The wisdom of the story points forward, from the birth of humanity to its present audience; but to arrive there the denouement must go backwards, into the most ancient strata of the psyche. So the economy of the story begins to reveal itself. It is the economy of dreams, the weird algebra of the night.

Now Coyote begins to hunt. Day after day Coyote hunts – hunts his animals, the animals of land. Deer, rabbit, antelope. Night after night those nether mouths devour the food Coyote brings. Crunch grind, grind crunch under those rabbitskin skirts. Is it a parody of Shoshonean courtship? The women continue to eat, and meat, after all, is meat. Once Coyote tentatively tries some foolishness with his finger and almost has it snapped off.

Now, myths work by compensation and by transformation. So, Coyote doesn't flee the land of the women with vaginal teeth, he pacifies it. If these insatiable women with two mouths want food, then to starve them would be to starve himself of his sexual project. To starve the story too, and leave it issueless. How can one come out of two? Can Male and Female join to create one child? How can life, nourishment, renewal come out of death, the killing of animals for food? The story of the birth of humanity must also be a story about hunting. Coyote must leave Wolf, Water Girl must leave her mother, humankind differentiate itself from nature, the Amazons leave behind their hunt and take up the tools of women, Coyote return to the land of men. But the wombs that should issue life take it instead, grinding it up with those awful teeth. The wickiup is the site of death, a charnel house; the signs of the story must be reversed, the hut must become a nursery of new life. Everything is upside-down and it is Coyote's great project to turn it right. The women try to seal Coyote in, to keep him from escaping. He climbs out the only aperture left, the smoke hole.

But Coyote is never at a loss. He is the inventor, the great improvisor. What's needed here is a tool. A substitute for that phallus Coyote is never foolish enough to use. So he experiments. He tries the bones of rabbits and the women snap them off. He tries the bones of deer and they destroy them.

He tries the bones of antelope and they are obliterated. At last he tries the neck-bone of the mountain sheep, that animal most difficult to hunt, which, on its peaks, mediates between earth and sky. The women crack their nether teeth on the mountain sheep's neck-bone and Coyote, in a nice sadistic detail, rubs them smooth with the wild mountain rosebush, thorny flower of the heights. He has conquered the cannibal women with their own hunger and lust.

The lesson is, if there is going to be Culture, the first thing to do is to tame the women.

But the next thing to do is tame the men.

The Water Jug

All night long, while Coyote slept, the women were working on something. They were hatching some plot. What they were doing was weaving a water jug, the sort of thing someone would carry on a journey. One night Coyote dreamed they were dropping babies into that jug and stoppering them up. Having solved one riddle, Coyote had only engendered a new one. Limp, exhausted, he thought it was a terrible thing for women to have teeth between their legs, but maybe it was even more terrible when they didn't.

The Journey

They were standing in front of the wickiup, their faces cracked in grins, cackling, showing him the road. It was time for Coyote to leave. He had emerged from the womb of the wickiup reborn himself, ready to be the father of humanity. So he hoisted the wicker bottle on his back and staggered off into the fresh morning light. The sun was glittering in the water on either side of the causeway as he walked. Far above him flew Water Girl snapping off the necks of mallards with her twat.

First Coyote went north, up into the broken peaks of the Jarbidge range and through twisted passes into the Owyhee country. From inside the willow bottle he could hear the sound of many voices, muted and faint, twittering like birds, a memory of that watery world he had left behind. Around the Quinn River he sat down. The women had warned him not to open the jug until he was home, but he longed to find out who the singers were. He tried to open the stopper of the jug just a crack, to get a glimpse inside. But the minute he pried the stopper open, out of the darkness flew many powerful men and women, who scattered in all directions with their bows and cradleboards, and he quickly replaced the stopper again.

Then he set out to the west. He trudged across the barren waste of the Black Rock Desert, the sun behind him, his hunchback shadow leading him onward. The bottle was still heavy, weighing him down. The singing inside was driving him crazy. He fell down at Pyramid Lake and sat on the hard ground watching the waves lap against the shore and the gulls wheeling against a few high, horsetail clouds. Again he couldn't stand it and opened the jug for a little peek and sat there bawling while he watched beautiful people in feathers and paint scatter in all directions before he had a chance to close the mouth of the bottle.

He hitched the willow bottle to his back again and went south, past the sink where the Humboldt loses itself in the desert sand, then down among the willows of the Walker River and past Mono Lake where strange towers of crystallized mineral rise along the salt shore and birds scream from their nests among the extinct volcanoes. He passed dead lava flows and steam rising from hot springs and thermal pools, then trudged on through the meadows of the Owens Valley with the looming scarp of the Sierra Nevadas on his right and the desert on his left. He passed Mount Whitney and headed east into the terrible jumble of rock and sand of Death Valley and his tongue was hanging out of his mouth from thirst. Then he entered the spiny wilderness of the Amargosa Desert, with its armies of Joshua trees waving their drunken arms. Somewhere out of Las Vegas he sat down. The songs coming out of the willow jug were very faint, and he wondered if the people inside were perishing. But when he opened the stopper to look, they flew out like bats and took off naked through the desert with lizard hooks in their hands and disappeared into the caves along the dry streambeds.

He went on. The sun hit against the naked rock. It rebounded from the desert in shimmering waves. He started to climb once more, up into the pines and aspen of the Cedar Breaks, and the air was thin and cold in his lungs as he came to the red earthen gash in the mountain. Then he turned his face north, dropping down into the desert again. But he didn't stop. His feet were torn. His balls were shriveled up. The water bottle was light now, almost weightless. He wondered if it was finally empty.

The sun was setting in a wall of fire on his left hand, his shadow streamed out to his right, grotesque, bent under the hollow jug, rippling across the bluffs. He kept the Schell Creek Mountains to his left, the Snakes to his right. Now to the east he could see the glittering, endless waste that was the Great Salt Lake Desert, with the water like a sheet of liquid flame. Then right up in front of him rose the Deep Creek range. The songs that came from the jug were not pretty songs anymore, but the dry, buzzing drone of medicine songs. He kept going. The red rays of the dead sun streamed out from the thunderhead forming to the west. The heat was still tremendous.

Coyote sat down on the desert floor. His shadow was immense as it flooded Ibapah Valley. He was the most curious creature who had ever lived. He had poked his nose into his own excrement and had looked up into the stars. He had smashed Wolf's utopia just to see what would happen. He'd scratched his balls and tried to screw his own daughters and juggled the eyes right out of his head. He had smelled the sharp smell of pine nuts roasting in the fall and had tried to fly with the cannibal geese. He had tricked everybody and been tricked himself and he had invented everything and lived a season with the women with vaginal teeth. He opened the jug for the last time. There were only a few people in it. They climbed out of the neck of the jug and he saw they were black and naked and covered with chalky dust. But they were his own children at last. And when he touched their arms he saw that under the dust they were sinewy and tough as mountain mahogany. He watched his children disappear into the scrub and wondered what manner of people they would be.

3   DUST PEOPLE

West of the Rocky Mountains, in those arid lands that were once called the Great American Desert, there was a wandering and horseless people made up of a half-dozen different groups, all related by a common root language and by a culture that is now called Shoshonean. They were Indians, of course, but so far removed were they in their nakedness from the "civilized" tribes to the east, the Mohawks, Shawnees, and Senecas, the Cherokees and others whose governments and leaders were still remembered by those who had come close to destroying them, or from the mounted warrior tribes of the plains, that they were almost classed as another species. "Diggers" was the name contemptuously applied to them, for their everpresent tool, the stick their women used to pry roots from the ground and with which men would skewer the rodents they subsisted upon – rats, ground squirrels, gophers. They were thieves. The trains of fur traders that came through their country watched them constantly following, begging. In the daylight the trappers would find a bucket missing, an ax, a bag of salt. The Indians stole the beaver traps out of the streams in which they'd been set. A trap would cost ten or twenty dollars in St. Louis. In the wilderness it was irreplaceable.

In 1833, somewhere near the Carson Sink, Joe Walker massacred twenty-five or thirty "Shoshokoes" who had been following his train and stealing traps. The Indians were unarmed and howled piteously on the opposite bank of the river. When the mountain men chased them, they ran away like frightened sheep. Even the names the travelers gave them were wrong. They were called Snakes, Shoshokoes, Land Pitches. Diggers. One traveler described the Paiute and "Land Pitches."

They wear no clothing of any description – build no shelters. They eat roots, lizards, and snails. . . . They provide nothing for future wants. And when the lizard and snail and wild roots are buried in the snows of winter, they are said to retire to the vicinity of timber, dig holes in the form of ovens in the steep sides of the sand hills, and having heated them to a certain degree, deposit themselves in them, and sleep and fast till the weather permits them to go abroad again for food.

They were subhuman, hibernating like reptiles or bears, scavenging like carrion eaters. After a severe winter the ground outside of these ovens was said to be strewn with the unburied bodies of the dead, while the half-starved survivors crawled among them on hands and knees, eating grass. In the spring they were hunted, weak and helpless as they were, and when caught were fattened and taken to Santa Fe to be sold as slaves.

And always there were the stories the whites would tell of what these people would stoop to eat – rats, lizards, insects, grass – as if humanity lay only on the other side of hunger. Wagon trains bogged down in the deserts jettisoned supplies, sacks of flour, beans. The Indian children threw the beans into the air and the elders daubed their blankets with the flour that they believed was the white man's medicine paint. We didn't know that stuff was grub, one Paiute remembered. When these Indians rode, they rode badly. A horse or a mule run off from a wagon train was meat, not transportation. But among all these people was one band more unfortunate by far than any, rejected even by their own kind.

..

They were the poorest of the poor. Long before the whites first came to the Great Basin these people were outcasts, despised and feared· by other tribes. When Escalante found the Utes fishing and hunting for birds on Utah Lake they told him of these Indians living to the west, in the deserts around an inland sea. The Utes called them poor people. They said they were a race of sorcerers.

They produced nothing permanent, had no real villages, no tribal communities. They did not know what it was to own a piece of ground or a sum of money. They might own a song or a bow. The men did not own their own wives. In the time of the Spaniards, when they were starving, husbands tried to sell their wives to the Ute slavers. The women just ran away and came home. In winter they dressed in rabbitskin robes that came only to their knees. Walking through the snow to forage or hunt, they would squat to pull the robe around them for warmth. Almost always they were barefoot. In their telling of the origin myth they would point to an island in the Great Salt Lake as the home of the women with vaginal teeth. Their ancestor was the last to come out of Coyote's water bottle. He was covered with dust. But he was tougher than other people. They said he was bulletproof. Like other bands, they were named by strangers: *kusippih* meant ashes, dry earth in Shoshone. They were the *kusiutta,* the Dust People.

In the springtime, they came out of the winter camps along the streams and in the canyons where the foothills of the mountains had given a little protection from the cold and the drifting snow. They had lived all winter on stored foods and what small animals they could catch, and they were hungry for green things. They scratched into the snowy ground for the first roots, the first green plants, carved seed and squaw cabbage, waded into the marshes for the new shoots of cattail. Then their wandering began, the annual circle that measured their lives. They moved from valley to valley, harvesting the seeds, competing with the birds and rodents among whom they lived for nourishment. Every valley had a seed that reached its moment of ripeness and had to be taken within a day or two before it burst its casing and scattered. As they went from camp to camp, erecting the brush shelters that were their only homes, they hunted small game or scooped up the few fish of desert springs in their hands. Deer were rare. There were rabbits, and once or twice a year the small bands would group together for a drive, surrounding the frightened creatures and forcing them into the long rabbit nets where they were clubbed to death by boys. They did not hunt the rarer antelope yearly, since to do so would decimate them, but waited for their shamans to tell them when the time was right, and then the shamans dreamed the antelope out of the desert and drove them into rough pens across the mouth of a draw or a canyon wall. They kept traveling through the year, and they knew over eighty species of desert plants that

12

gave seeds, berries, roots, greens. Their one native dance was the round dance, the dance that made the seeds grow.

In the fall of the year, if the pine nut crop had been good, there was a momentary respite. The groves were dotted with fires and the sharp smells of burning pine and roasting nuts. While they harvested the nuts and prepared them for the long winter, roasting and grinding them into meal, they sang and gambled, courted, and made matches. At night the boys crawled into their rabbitskin blankets black with pine pitch and dust, full, for once, on pine nut soup. In a few days they would head back across the desert to scout their winter camp. The Dust People were masters of a kind of survival where the margin between life and starvation was thin as a hair.

Before 1847 white trappers had been only occasional wayfarers, gaunt and thirsty men wandering up out of the desert into the Dust People's country, or trading with more prosperous tribes on its edges. Then came the first permanent settlements at the border of their territory. The Mormons fixed themselves in the Salt Lake Valley against the foothills of the Wasatch Mountains where the Dust People had sometimes ventured to hunt deer. They built villages and sawmills along streams where the Dust People had camped and plowed up the deserts for wheat farms where once the Dust People had harvested crickets.

..

May 9, 1859, Camp No. 7, Sulphur Springs. . . . About 125 miles out from Camp Floyd, at the western edge of the Great Salt Lake Desert, Captain James H. Simpson of the U.S. Army Corps of Topographical Engineers, surveying a new wagon route through the Great Basin, made this entry in his journal:

We have to-day seen a number of Go-shoot Indians. They are most wretched looking creatures, certainly the most wretched I have ever seen, and I have seen great numbers in various portions of our country. . . .

I learn from Mr. Faust, the mail-agent at this point, that there are only about 200 Go-shoots all told of every age. They use, generally, the bow and arrow, there being only one gun to about 25 men. He represents them as of a thievish disposition, the mail company having lost by them about 12 head of cattle and as many mules. They steal them for food.

At sunset Simpson and some of his men walked out to see the Gosiute camp. The Gosiutes were wary and had stopped some distance from water, which they carried to their camp in willow jugs smeared with fir-gum.

Their only shelter was a circle of cedar branches about ten feet in diameter, which rose to four feet high in the direction from which the wind came. Inside the circle were men, women, and children, the men and women dressed in rabbitskin robes, the nursing infants naked. The Indians were cooking the meat the survey team had given them in a camp kettle. While the survey team watched, a hunter came in with his game: a number of rats stuck under the thong around his waist. The old woman who tended the fire singed the hair of the rats and rubbed them clean with a pine knot, then gutted them with her finger, stripped the entrails, which she stuffed back into the paunch, and threw the rats into the pot.

Simpson did not try the rats, but he did try a kind of cake made of seeds and roots. To him it looked precisely like a cake of cow dung, and when he tasted it, he quickly spit it out. The military party was amused to see the women slyly tucking the hickory shirts they gave them under their rabbitskins, "their whole demeanor representing that they are a suspicious, secretive set."

For Simpson the Dust People were an object of study and a proof of the Divine Plan. All history, all geography, and the races of humanity themselves were a confirmation of that plan that was culminating at that moment in the conquest of the globe by the European race. This was the opinion of Professor Arnold Guyot, late of Neuchâtel, later of Princeton, for whom Simpson had had the honor of naming a not inconsiderable range of mountains south of the Great Salt Lake. It was Guyot's theory that climatic conditions, as shaped by world geography (and, of course, Divine Plan) had rendered Europe the final destination of the highest civilization. The last stage of the progress of the world toward enlightenment was to be reached with the conquest of North America, when the European, "the man of ripened age, who reflects upon men and things" – someone, perhaps, like Professor Guyot – "analyzes the causes, and seeks to understand the lessons of the spectacle the world presents" and joins the young, white, American "full of fire and energy" to redeem the rest of the globe.

The impoverished people before Simpson were representatives of those iron laws of geography and moral history that one saw sketched out in plates v. and vi. of Professor Guyot's book, where, ranged in descending order from the true Caucasian type, and "all those perfections the chisel of a Phidias or a Praxiteles has combined upon a single head," we at last come to "those figures which we always behold with . . . secret uneasiness," an uneasiness "that would threaten to grow into disgust, were not the feeling lost in pity still more profound, and in the charity of a Christian heart." Far from God, farther still, perhaps, from Neuchâtel or Princeton, the Go-shoots seemed to be one of Guyot's descriptions come to life, "a melancholy, cold and insensible race. 'Foreign to our hopes, our joys, our griefs.'" Could one imagine, Guyot asked his audiences in Boston, the thousands of elegant nothings displayed in our drawing-rooms among the Indians of the Rocky Mountains, sheltered by the few branches which form their wretched huts? Indeed, had Raphael been born among such miserable people, would he ever have given his admirable masterpieces to the world? No Raphaels here. Just misery, poverty, degradation. And an opportunity for trained observation.

Two days after he had visited the Gosiute camp at Sulphur Springs, Simpson came upon a group of what he called Root-Diggers on the east slope of Antelope Valley. At first the Indians were afraid to come near, but some bread was given to an old woman and she signed the others to approach. Simpson was touched to see this famished woman, "the most lean, wretched looking object" it had ever been his lot to see, deal out the bread first to the little child at her side, then to the others. When all had been fed she took the small balance for herself. "It is refreshing, however, in all their degradation, to see the mother studiously careful of her little one, by causing it to nestle under her rabbit-skin mantle." He visited one of the wick-iups but the feces piled up around it caused his stomach to turn, and he beat a hasty retreat. The quantity of feces was no doubt caused, thought Simpson, by the vegetable, innutritious character of the Indians' food.

So Captain Simpson forged on, minutely examining the geology, the plants, the fauna of the Great Basin, instructing his photographer to take likenesses of one or another of the desolate people he found living in the desert, recording barometric readings, and surveying the route for the wagon road. He was firmly established in his belief that God and Geography had come together at this moment, in this place; that it was here that the Plan of the Great I Am was being worked out. "To what people," the philosophical Guyot had asked, "shall it belong to carry out this work into reality? The law of history replies, to a new people. And to what continent? The geographical march of civilization tells us, to a new continent west of the Old World – to America." America lay glutted with its vegetable wealth, unworked, solitary. Meantime, the Indians, the primitive owners of these vast territories, had shown themselves incapable or careless of work. Upon a soil able to support millions in plenty, a few scattered inhabitants led a wretched existence in the bosom of the wilderness. Happy Captain Simpson should have been, as he slogged through the desert, not to know that in England a man was working on the final draft of a book that would forever lay waste, by its method and its intellectual power, to the cheerful certitudes of the Guyots of the world that they were on God's side. In *On the Origin of the Species* there was no God's side to be on. There was no plan. The light of grace that gleamed at the end of the continent justifying the westward thrust of the Europeans, their massacres, and their appropriations, was a fiction of their own devising.

When Captain Simpson made his survey report on the wagon route the California gold strike at Sutter's Mill was ten years old. That very summer came the gold and silver strikes in the Comstock. New freight and mail routes cut through the heart of the Gosiute country. The freighters and mail contractors dammed up the springs around which the Indians had lived, killed the few fish they had scooped out of the water. The white men's mules and cattle ate the grass whose seeds the Dust People had gathered for centuries. Simpson and Professor Guyot went on with their pious speculations about the Future of America. Uprooted by the collapse of an environment on which they had had a slender hold at best, the Dust People became beggars at the settlements, gleaning the grain left over on Mormon threshing floors, waiting for scraps from the tables of mining town boarding houses, a bucket of offal from the slaughterhouse.

4   EVERYMAN'S INDIAN

A man came upon an Indian in the forest. Prithee,
said the man, whose Indian are you? Said the
Indian to the man, Nay, Sir, whose Indian are you?
Early American tale

They were two weeks out from St. Joseph, Missouri, and the journey had taken on the quality of an hallucination. The passengers in the coach were coated with dust. Their perspiration dried before it reached the dead, still air. Except for the champing and blowing of the poor, unwatered mules, there wasn't a sound. Not a sigh, not a whisper; not a buzz or whirr of wings or the distant pipe of a bird. The sun beat down with a dead, blistering malignity. There was no breeze, not even a shred of cloud. The Confidential Secretary found himself listening for the lost souls who must have peopled that dead air.

In the middle of the day the canteens went dry. The alkali dust cut through the passengers' lips and persecuted their eyes and at last their noses began to bleed uncontrollably. The Secretary gave his dust-coated pocket watch what he thought was a good long rest, then unsnapped its case. It was a mistake. The hands of the watch had scarcely moved at all. There was no time here. Only dust.

It was at one of the string of desert stations that hung tenuously to that hair-thin road that the Secretary must have first seen it. A handful of brittle bones wrapped in filthy rags, long dirty hair, and an iron gray, shriveled face in which there was neither fear nor anger nor anything else but hunger. It was a man, and he was begging.

There may have been others with this poor figure, hidden away from the spring where the Company watered its stock, their camp a wall of brush, a scavenged kettle, a rusty ladle, a few rags begged from the stage passengers or the men who kept the station. These were the Goshoots, the native inhabitants of this hell.

Small, lean, "scrawny" creatures; in complexion a dull black like the ordinary American Negro; their faces and hands bearing dirt which they had been hoarding and accumulating for months, years, and even generations, according to the proprietor; a silent, sneaking, treacherous-looking race; taking note of everything, covertly . . . and betraying no sign in their countenance; indolent, everlastingly patient and tireless, like all other Indians; prideless beggars . . . hungry, always hungry, and yet never refusing anything that a hog would eat, though often eating what a hog would decline.

They had no villages, no farms, no homes. Their only shelter was a rag cast on a bush to keep off some of the snow. When you asked one of these Indians if he believed in a Great Spirit he would show something which almost amounted to emotion, thinking it was whiskey to which you were referring.

And they were killers. The Secretary heard with his own ears of an attack on a stage, the driver mortally wounded, his passenger taking over the reins and outracing the howling savages. One would as soon expect the rabbits to fight as the Goshoots, and yet after living off the refuse of the station a few months, come some dark night and they would burn down the buildings and ambush the fleeing men. The Goshoots – descended from the same gorilla or kangaroo or Norway rat as the Bushmen – like the other Indians of America called up in the Secretary only nausea. They deserved pity – and they could have his, at a distance. Nearer by, they never got anybody's.

The station men hitched up a new team, the passengers brushed a few final clouds of dust from their rumpled clothes and got into the coach, the driver gave a snap to the lines and they were on the road once again. The Confidential Secretary went on to Carson City. Went on to San Francisco, to the Sandwich Islands. Went on to become Mark Twain, that showy public edifice haunted so uneasily by the ghost of Sam Clemens. He taught himself to be everybody's pet Bad Boy, the lovable prankster in the heart of the Victorian household, smoking, Sabbath breaking, swearing, telling dirty jokes. He was, if he had only known it, playing a part like the Goshoot's own god, Coyote. Like Coyote, he spoke in every accent, mimicked every voice. He pranced and howled for his public, lisped and made a fool of himself and on the pages that flowed from his pen created whole tribes of jokers and fools in his image. He was a public shaman, a wizard whose magic was the word, who destroyed whole worlds of cultural pretension with his laughter, his bad behavior. But he could not heal his people. He could not suck the evils from them or go off on a journey to find their lost souls. The greed, the violence, the patriotic obscenities that were driving the chariot of Imperial America remained. He was no wizard, but only a pale, counterfeit version of Coyote after all.

Once, however, he had found his voice. It was in a book about an orphan boy and a runaway slave. He ditched that literary bore Tom Sawyer in the fourth chapter and set out with Huck Finn and Miss Watson's Jim on a raft down the Mississippi and discovered something true in himself. It was a hard book to write, and he had to put it off again and again. In the summer of 1884, the year of the publication of *Huckleberry Finn,* he began work on a new book.

He sent Huck, Tom, and Jim on a new adventure. They lit out for the Territory, as Huck had talked about at the conclusion of the book that bore his name. Tom was all mad for Indians. "Why Jim, they're the noblest human beings that's ever been in the world. . . . An Injun is *all* honor. It's what they're *made* of. . . . They're just all generousness and unstingeableness. And brave? Why, they ain't afraid of anything." Tom had gotten it all from Cooper's novels, of course, but the man who had once gone to the Comstock as his brother's confidential secretary knew better. Sioux or Mohican, the Indians were all Goshoots underneath, and the fun of the book would be shoving poor Tom up against the real thing. But the book wasn't any fun. It went on listlessly for nine chapters, and then Twain abandoned it. A book of false trails and palid characters and unresolved questions. Unfinished, saltless, wrong. And, finally, disturbing. For at the heart of the book was something left unsaid.

The words that had made Mark Twain's fortune in the end betrayed him. What Coyote knew, the horrible joys of violence and sex, his apprentice could not let himself admit. The slaves among whom he had grown up, whose children he had played with in the house in Hannibal, were too near for Twain to demonize, and he spent his maturity trying to purge himself of the racism he had inherited. But the Indian was too far away from him, too dirty, too impoverished. And too close to some deep thing in him, some terrible hunger and rage.

He was always a Boy, yes. But it was as if the sign of his Boyhood was this terrible silence around sex. Once he had gone into Injun Joe's cave with Becky Thatcher, but he had not illuminated that darkness. The questionable jokes, the schoolboy-like secret manuscripts, were his whistling in the dark. He always came back into the sunlight grateful and gaping. For him there was no love possible to write about except the distant, awed puppy love of a Boy for "someone's big sister."

She had read considerable many books, and knowed as much as most any girl, and was just as pretty as ever she could be, and live. But she warn't no prettier than she was good, and all the tribe doted on her.

This was Huck Finn's description of seventeen-year-old Peggy Mills, of Twain's abandoned manuscript. Despite the tone of comic rusticity, Peggy Mills is just another sentimental heroine of the Victorian novel. But as in all such perfection, there was something, underneath, that willed its own destruction. What Wolf builds Coyote breaks for sheer joy and spite. Such terrible polarities cannot be maintained.

So the Indians run off with Peggy and her little sister and Jim. What they do to Peggy is too awful to be told: there are some pegs driven into the ground, a bloody scrap of Peggy's dress. Clues that yield no victim and no criminal. The book comes up again and again against a silence, a gap. And finally it cannot be written at all.

..

He is old. The Boy is dying. He has seen financial disaster, the deaths of his wife and a favorite daughter, the sickness and death of another daughter, the horrors of the Philippine War. A darkness spreads over him. The things he has left out of his books have always tormented him. "They burn in me; & they keep multiplying & multiplying; but now they can't ever be said. And besides, they would require a library – & a pen warmed-up in hell."

He paces and plays endless games of billiards with himself, and what he writes is often supressed. He poses in his Oxford robes, and invites a troop of admiring pubescent girls to join him in the billiard room. He calls them his angel-fish. Old Coyote, desexed by age, lying down with the lambs. But in his dreams a man comes to him. He is starving. He is filthy. The man or creature or thing opens his mouth, but no sound comes out, he dumbly makes words in an appeal, as if there is no language for what he wants.

5   ANTELOPE JAKE

Throughout the Great Basin the decade following the first white settlements was a time of troubles. Settlers pushed deeper and deeper into the Indian territories, cutting off supplies of food, driving away or killing the game, forcing the native peoples into ever-narrowing areas of open land. Stage and freight lines forged their way through the desert, appropriating the few springs for their stations, driving stock out on the land to eat the grasses the People depended on. An Indian agent described the increasingly desperate situation of the Great Basin Indians bluntly. "We have eaten up their grass and utterly deprived them of its rich crop of seed. . . . Now there is nothing left for them to eat but ground squirrels and pis-ants."

In desperation, the Indians turned to raiding. Sheep and cattle were driven off, soldiers and settlers killed. Whites were not slow to retaliate. In 1851, an expedition of Mormons from the Tooele Valley massacred every man in a camp of Gosiutes. With no guns, with no war horses, with no plans, with only their bows and arrows and a few simple ideas of what it was to hunt men instead of antelope, the Dust People rose up, burning the mail stations and killing the stock.

In March 1859, Indian subagent Robert Jarvis went out to call the Indians in to talk. When he got to Ibapah, on the western slope of the Deep Creek Mountains, he found about a hundred Indians waiting for him. They were starving. The rest were afraid to come in for fear the summons was a trap.

On the second of April Jarvis ordered a steer killed and held a council with seventy-three warriors. He "elected," as he put it, an old man called

Arra-won-nets head chief and Ka Vana subchief "without any opposition."

Jarvis found that the Indians had turned to farming. They had no tools, no help. They had put out thirty or forty acres of wheat, turning up the ground with sticks. Jarvis spoke to them, told them that the Great Father wanted to treat them as his children, and would make them a good farm. He said that he had heard of many cattle and mules being stolen by them, and that they had stopped the mail and fired upon agents carrying letters to the Great Father. Jarvis said that he would forgive them, but if he heard of anything of the kind occurring again, the Great Father would send many soldiers out who would not leave one of them alive. The Indians agreed to his speech, and Jarvis had another beef killed and gave out some presents. On April third, the Indians left for Deep Creek.

That night the band that had committed the depredations came in. The next morning Jarvis met the renegades in council for over an hour. He and the other two white men impressed upon them the need to abandon their roving life and take up the peaceful pursuit of agriculture. Jarvis was pleased to say there was not a single objection made.

But the farms and equipment the Indians were promised never came. The tillable land in the desert was occupied by whites. So the peace did not last. The soldiers sent to guard the mail and freight lines hunted down innocent bands of Indians, wiping them out for sport. The Indians fought back. Stages were attacked, their drivers killed. In Egan Canyon a wagon train was surrounded. The Indians cut the tugs of the harnesses and ran off the horses and mules. The men and women were killed and the children had their brains dashed out on the wagon hubs. Government troops, under Albert Sidney Johnston, marched out of their base at Camp Floyd in the Oquirrh Mountains and headed across the desert to punish the Indians.

..

His Indian name has been lost. His father Kutanzip – Exploding Firewood – was a shaman of the Antelope Valley Indians. Already the young man was a famous hunter. Working alone, he stalked the antelope in disguise, lying in wait near a spring or water hole and depending on his own skill. He had used this skill to run off the horses and mules of the mail line, and once, in retaliation for the butchery of a camp of defenseless Pahvants and Gosiutes at Coyote Springs, he had taken part in a raid on a coach station where four soldiers and a hostler were killed. Now, a renegade on the run from the whites, he had killed an antelope at a desert spring. He was beginning to butcher it, when the young white man found him.

This white man was a Mormon named Elijah Wilson – Nick Wilson. Just short of his twelfth birthday he had run away from the frontier harshness of the Mormon settlement of Tooele for the romantic life with the Shoshone Chief Washakie's band. Later, Wilson had left the band and became a pony express rider through these same desert wastes; he had seen the aftermath of the massacre of the emigrant train at Egan Canyon. As an army scout he had led the soldiers of General Albert Sidney Johnston to an isolated Indian camp beside a lake and watched the Indian children trying to hide in the bullrushes while the soldiers attacked. By the battle's end the soldiers had killed everyone in the camp, even the dogs. Now Wilson called out to the young Indian surprised over the dead antelope. He spoke in Shoshone. He called the Indian "friend." It is here that the Gosiute version of the story begins.

The White Man had a paper with him. He told the hunter that he had camped out too many nights, and that the white people had captured him, had taken him for a son. The paper that young Nick Wilson held, is, in the Indian way of telling the story, the treaty that would forever bind the Dust People to the White Man's law. In the story it takes on a foreboding presence. It becomes the White Man's magic, sealing the Gosiute's fate. "You are captured," the White Man says. And that is all that needs to be said. Everything is over.

Wilson told the young hunter to go to his home and tell the Indians what had happened to him, then to go to the fort at Ibapah, so that the white man would not kill him off, but would tell him what to do. So the captured man went back to his camp. And then, as he had promised, he returned to the fort.

Spending so many nights he then arrived. He wore a stolen red sash as a belt. He arrived wearing the belt. He came down there walking jauntily with a hop. It was down there where the sumac grows. It must have some name there. . . . The soldiers were holding guns in their hands. They were ready to shoot him on the spot. He kept going anyway. He had on their sash, the one which was stolen. . . .

The chief of the soldiers stood there. He looked fierce. There were two yellow things on him. They talked for awhile. . . . [His uniform] was very blue.

"You will remain here and be chief. Because you killed the antelope then, the White Men will call you Antelope Jake." The one standing here [the commander] he said . . . "[You will] remain here," he said. "Any of the people who stay [here]

22

will come and eat with you," he said. "Maybe they will come with you and farm," he said. "Maybe they will thus cultivate hay seeds," he said. "Maybe they will grow all sorts of things." The White Man spoke that way.

I have seen no white account that mentions that stolen sash. But the soldiers who saw the young man from Antelope Springs walk boldly into their camp knew where it had come from.

It was years after this that the full story of Antelope Jake's war against the whites would come out. By that time Antelope Jake was an old man, living at Ibapah. A rancher named Jim Sharp had heard rumors for years that there was more to the tales of the killings of the soldiers and hostler at Canyon Station than he knew. And there was another story he wanted to find out about, which concerned five mail riders who had been ambushed near Simpson Springs in the time of the Indian troubles. One day Sharp took four cans of tomatoes out to an old Indian who was herding sheep for him. The gift of the tomatoes loosened the old Indian's tongue, and he told Sharp the story of the massacre of the Indian camp at Coyote Springs and the retaliatory raid on Canyon Station. Then he told him another story, and this, too, concerned the man the whites called Antelope Jake.

It was fall, and Jake and his band had been camping in Deep Creek Valley for their annual hunt. The men and young women had gone off for six days, leaving the old women and girls, including Jake's sixteen-year-old daughter Suzy, to take care of the children. One day five white men on horseback leading a train of mules came to the camp and demanded meat, but the women did not understand them, and when the whites pointed to a deer carcass the women shook their heads. Then one of the men looked into a wickiup and saw the girls. Years later, when Sharp wrote of it, he said what had happened didn't even need telling.

When Jake and the rest of the band returned, the women of the camp told what the white men had done. With no horses and armed only with their bows, six of the Indians followed the mail riders through the desert. The white men were mounted, armed with pistols. Still the Indians went after them, keeping out of sight. The Indians caught up with four of the riders at the foot of Lava Mountain, and were driven back. Still they continued to follow. They waited until the white men camped, then went ahead, and the next day, when a heavy snow began to fall, they ambushed them in a dry ravine at the foot of Dugway Mountain.

..

Out at the desert fort in the Deep Creek Valley, two fundamentally different notions of power were contending with each other. For the white man,
power is a function of some hierarchical structure; it is not in the gold
epaulets of the general, but in the rank they stand for. For the Gosiutes,
power is essentially a species of spiritual potency. The attempts of Indian
agents and army officers to give this foreign name "chief" to those who did
not seek it or need it were finally fatuous. The power that anyone might
have was not, for the Dust People, political, but a power of vision. Young
men would go to the mountains or a cave where there were pictographs
and receive their dreams. They fasted and painted their bodies with white
clay and waited. Perhaps Elk would come and give doctoring powers, or
Water Baby would give power in war. Or the dwarf Mountain Man with
his tiny bow and arrows, who wore a cape in the summer, went naked in
winter, might teach the use of herbs or give hunting power. Sometimes a
young man had dreamed the same dream as his father and inherited his
medicine. Then the father's power left him to reside in his son. For power
was a kind of substance, a magic. As the young man who had killed the antelope came into the fort with that jaunty hop he gathered his medicine
about him. He wore a stolen sash that for him may have been a talisman, a
fetish appropriated from a powerful race.

But power was not only in things, but in songs, in dances. For what the
spirit-creatures taught in dreams – their powers and secrets – were passed
down in dance and song. That is the meaning of that jaunty hop. When the
young man entered that fort among the guns of his enemies, I believe that
he came singing and dancing.

Antelope Jake returned home to tell the Dust People to lay down their
bows and go up to Ibapah to take up farming. He told them that he had
been made chief, that he would now not be afraid to do anything. That he
would go back without being afraid, that he would even mingle with the
whites, that they would be his friends. Perhaps Antelope Jake simply gave
himself up to the superior magic, to the white man's way. But there is also
in the Gosiute tradition a tragic acquiesence to a new fate, as they recollect
Antelope Jake's telling of it:

"Our fighting is making us become extinct. . . . At Pasama the White Men killed
lots of Indians," he said. "Then they killed some more between the mountains.
They killed lots of Indians there," he said. It was there that the White Man ate some
girls after killing the Indians. . . ." They ate us after they killed us. They threw us
away after they killed us. There is nothing we can do about it," he said. "[We] don't

have any guns and therefore can't do anything. [We] only have bows. [We] can't kill anything out there," he said.

He remembered those girls, raped, "eaten," in the hills. The old life was over. It would never come back. They should do what the white people told them to do. Maybe then the boys would grow up to become young men, the girls would grow up to become young ladies, some would grow old and pass away.

"They were rubbing us out," he said. "We are becoming nothing. There is only a handful of us left. I myself also laid down my gun, remaining here and no longer fighting, like the White Man told us," he said. That's what he said. Antelope Jake.

Maude Moon, who told this story in 1967, ended it in the traditional formula: That's it. The rat's tail fell off. The formula kept the story in the Indian world, in the world of Wolf, of Coyote, of Cottontail. But it was a world that even as Antelope Jake spoke, had begun to die.

In January of 1863 federal troops massacred 250 Northwestern Shoshone camped along the Bear River near Franklin, Idaho – men, women, and children. The officers watched while the troops raped the women in the midst of the slaughter. In May of the same year, the Sacramento *Union* was praising the gallant Captain S. P. Smith for massacring 53 Gosiutes without the loss of a single man. The *Union* regreted only that he could not have been at the Bear River fight. In mid-June Smith killed 10 more Indians at Government Springs. The end of Indian resistance had come.

On 12 October 1863, the Gosiutes signed a treaty that gave the whites the right to build mines, mills, and ranches in their territory and guaranteed the safety of the mails and telegraph lines and of the railroad that was soon to arrive. The treaty gave the president of the United States the right to determine when the Indians should abandon their roaming life and become stock raisers and farmers on reservations. The Indians signed away their old life for a thousand dollars down and a thousand dollars a year in goods and cattle for the next two decades. They could hardly have understood what this paper meant, except that by it they were promised they would not starve.

There is white man's history and there is Indian's history. The white man is concerned with dates, with order, with the links between cause and effect. The Indian is concerned with meaning that flows backward and forward at once on the roads of time. It is a mistake to think that the truth is somewhere between both histories, that Antelope Jake, whoever he was, fits neatly into a space where the two merge. The two histories, the two truths, never met; between them, an old way was virtually destroyed. Out in the western desert, two visions of history and two visions of power had collided, and the Indians' had been vanquished. For the young man who killed the antelope at the spring and who walked through the snow with his bow to avenge the rape of the Gosiute girls, the old life was over. Now he entered the white man's world with a white man's name and wearing a white man's sash. He came into that world out of necessity, but he took his own medicine with him.

6 BAPTISM IN THE DESERT

And he had caused the cursing to come
upon them, yea, even a sore cursing, because
of their iniquity. For behold, they had
hardened their hearts against him, that they
had become like unto a flint; wherefore, as
they were white, and exceedingly fair and
delightsome, that they might not be enticing
unto my people the Lord God did cause a skin
of blackness to come upon them.
The Book of Mormon, 2 Nephi 5:21

To the European settlers who first entered the Americas, the native peoples presented an enigma. Who were they? Whence had they come? The Indians were too ignorant, too poor, too superstitious to be like the whites; yet they were too fundamentally intelligent, their ancient mounds too fine, to be anything but – though sadly fallen away. Were they related through some distant ancestry? Were they, perhaps, Visigoths? Or Welsh? The Book of Mormon, among other things, sought to account for the native inhabitants of the New World. That remarkable relic of the millenarianism of the Burnt Over District, with its context of nineteenth-century quackery, backwoods folklore, homespun gnosticism, all strained through Joseph Smith's fertile mind, adopted the then-popular thesis that the native peoples of this hemisphere were in fact displaced Hebrews. Posited in its revelatory pages was a myth of origin based on the adventures of two bands, the Nephites and the Lamanites. At one time they had been a single people, but the Lamanites had turned against God, and for this sin were cursed with a "skin of blackness." With the decampment of the God-fearing and industrious followers of Nephi, the backsliding Lamanites sank into a kind of preindustrial sloth, and because of the curse upon them "they did become an idle people, full of mischief and subtlety, and did seek in the wilderness for beasts of prey." Now for many ages (and many pages) would Lamanites and Nephites be at odds, and a good part of that sacred text would be the story of their wars and entanglements.

Thus the Latter-day Saints were living inheritors of biblical epic: indeed, by their sufferings, their prophecies, their daily lives, they carried on that tremendous past. Enfabled so, the very dust the Prophet Joseph's followers trod on – the hills and fields of upstate New York, of Iowa, Illinois, and Missouri, the straggling pioneer settlements beyond the Rocky Mountains – became holy ground. And so the poor Indians, loitering around the settlements, begging, sometimes sighted traveling across the sagebrush flats with their gathering baskets and battered cooking pots, were in fact the co-bearers with the Mormons of that sacred history. But was it sufficient for the Saints to live out their destiny among the scattered and fallen descendants of the Lamanites? The sacred calling of the Mormons laid upon them another obligation. For every curse carries appended to it the terms of its expunction. Repentance will bring restoration.

And then shall they rejoice; for they shall know that it is a blessing unto them from the hand of God; and their scales of darkness shall begin to fall from their eyes; and many generations shall not pass away among them, save they shall be a white and a delightsome people.

Established in their western Wilderness, surrounded by the remnants of this ancient people who came to their doors to beg or who drove off their stock or who simply did their best to ignore them, the Mormons faced a dilemma unlike that of other pioneers. Policy – whether to feed the Indians or to fight them – was constrained by theology. Sometimes the results were remarkable.

Jacob Hamblin, a settler in the beleaguered little fortress-town of Tooele, on the eastern edge of the Great Salt Lake, went off on an expedition to punish some Gosiute thieves. Hamblin and his company tracked the Indians in a light snow, but when, hidden in ambush, he had one of the Indians in his sights, his rifle misfired. The arrows the Indian shot at him struck his gun, went through his hat, his coat, and vest. Yet he was not harmed. He later learned that none of the others in the company had been able to fire their weapons either. The message was clear.

..

Out in the desert west of the Great Salt Lake, on the far side of a range of desert mountains called the Deep Creeks, is a place the Indians called Aipimpaa or "chalky water." It was there in 1874 that the Mormon William Lee came to baptize the Lamanites. For both Mormon and Indians significant events were always accompanied by signs and miracles and dreams. Thus the mass baptisms of the Gosiutes at Deep Creek were predicated on Mysteries.

Mormon and Indian legends merged in the recounting of a mysterious visitor who had appeared to a certain Toobuka, and who had announced that the time had come for the Indians to be "buried in the water," or baptized; the visitor said that the Mormons were the Indians' friends and had a book which told about their fathers, and that Brigham Young held communion with God and they must hear him. A second time and a third, mysterious visitors came to Toobuka, repeating the message exactly. Toobuka remembered that when two of these visitors had come, one had been considerably taller than the other.

No Mormon reading this account of the miraculous visitors could but thrill at the clues to the identity of these three mysterious men; for it was clear that they were the Three Nephites, deathless survivors of the lost Israelite tribes. The visits also impressed Toobuka, so much so that he gathered his followers and set off for Deep Creek, where he sent a messenger to the interpreter William Lee of Grantsville.

For the Indians, as for the Mormons, dreams were power. Indian shamans, too, laid on hands, and the ritual baths in springs and sweat lodges were healing processes and provided a prophylactic against evil. White was the color of power in Shoshonean ritual, and the men who sought visions daubed themselves in white clay. The Gosiutes were going to a place they knew well, to a stream they called chalky to be buried in the water and to emerge white. To have the things and the powers the *Mommonnee* had. "He may make them white over there," the Indians were saying. "I think I want to become white." They knew that when the white men came to them at least they were fed.

In early June 1874, in a driving rain, William Lee and three assistants held the Indians' noses and dunked them under the torrent at Deep Creek, where the bridge crosses the water. In an hour a hundred were so baptized into the faith. The women held out their babies to be baptized too, but the Mormons turned them away, since it was at eight years of age that they confirmed their own children.

The last to be baptized was Antelope Jake. For the shaman knew that when one's soul is lost, a doctor had to go himself to find it up the Dusty Path. Was that what he was doing, dying in the water? Trying to find his lost people's soul? There, in the icy spring currents of a creek the Indians called the Chalky Water, two strains of mythology merged, held together, perhaps, by something so slender as an accident of language.

But the Mormons' magic was no good. When they came out of the stream the Dust People were not white. The Mormons said some words and fed them only a little bit of bread William Lee had cooked in a dutch oven, and they went off to their homes in the valley shivering, bellies empty.

One after another those who walked back to their homes died of pneumonia or some other disease. Ten every morning and more at night, as they told it. Perhaps the water was too thick, the Indians said. It was yellow, greasy looking. Maybe it was too thick. They had listened to the Mormons and, once more, were fooled.

7   INTERLUDE

And – as far as the official white world was concerned – the Dust People simply disappeared. Writing in 1860, the English scholar-adventurer Richard Burton had predicted that, broken and dispersed by the late fighting, those few Gosiutes who had not abandoned the old wandering life, were doomed; like the Ghuzw of Arabia they would be forced to strengthen themselves by admitting the outcasts of other tribes, and would presently "become a mere banditti." Thirteen years later John Wesley Powell counted 256 Gosiutes in Utah. For every year after that the figure remained unchanged in the annual reports of the Office of Indian Affairs. After 1895, the Gosiutes vanish from the office's statistics. No one had bothered to count them. By the end of the century, they had become "a forgotten people."

They wanted to farm. This is what the whites had promised them, that they would let them have land, water, seed. Perhaps aboriginally they had begun some primitive farming, burning off a section of land and seeding it with wild grass. But the leap from their old ways of hunting and gathering was too much, the new tools too alien. Wheat they soon learned could be kept by the one who grew it, but they would not understand that potatoes belonged to the man who planted them: like the yampa root, potatoes grew underground. They belonged to everybody. At his father's ranch in Deep Creek Valley, Howard Egan watched a Gosiute irrigating by directing little streams of water with his fingers. A shovel stood up in the dirt behind him. The Indian did not want to use it. Soon whites began to press farther into the desert valleys and the Indians' Deep Creek farms were abandoned.

There was an Indian from Mason Valley in western Nevada the Dust People heard about after that. This Indian had had a dream. In the dream he learned that the Indians were supposed to dance for five days, that the Ghosts would come to help them and the whites would be destroyed. There would be seeds in the valleys and good hunting once more. By 1890 the Ghost Dance had spread throughout the West. (In Mason Valley even the Mormon farmers were dancing, for they too believed the world would soon end.) Some Indians came around and taught the Dust People the dances and the words to the songs, and they danced, but the Ghosts never came and the whites didn't go away and the Dust People forgot about the dream.

The Gosiutes used to go out to Skull Valley, sometimes, to see the people the Mormons had brought from across the western sea. The farm the Kanakas had out there wasn't a success. The Dust People would sit and listen to those Hawaiians plunking on their guitars and scraping their rasps and singing the sweet, mournful songs of their old islands. The Hawaiians weren't used to the climate and they sickened and died and longed for their homes. After a while leprosy broke out in that colony. The ones who hadn't already died or gone away began to perish. Finally there were only two old women locked up in the meeting house. They raised a flag when they wanted anything. Then they too were dead. The Dust People didn't go around there much after that.

The Dust People no longer gathered much for the pine nut harvest anymore, or to gamble or dance. Some of the young people wanted to live like white people. They worked for wages and lost their taste for the old foods. They were as lost as the children Walkara and the Utes had stolen to sell to the Mexicans when Antelope Jake had been a boy.

When Doctor Joseph Peck first saw Ibapah in March of 1917, it was a cluster of fifty wickiups covered with canvas and old blankets along the willows of Deep Creek. Behind the wickiups were the dirt-roofed government cabins, but the Gosiutes lived mostly in the wickiups and used the cabins for storing deerskins and sheep hides, dried apples, springs from old automobiles. In front of some of the wickiups were salvaged Ford touring cars, battered, missing tops and windscreens. The Gosiutes had bought them from the Wendover junkyards with the money they got for hauling the logs for the cabins.

For years the Dust People had lived on the charity of the Mormons, who had established farms for them at Deep Creek and in Skull Valley, fragile oases on opposite sides of the Great Salt Lake Desert. But the farms never produced enough, and the Gosiutes had to fight the white men for water. In those years Antelope Jake's name appears on a lawsuit seeking water for his people. By 1914, the Gosiutes were once again under government protection. A school was established at Deep Creek and a superintendent came to watch over the Dust People.

Amos Frank was an Ohio Presbyterian, a former schoolteacher and career employee of the Bureau of Indian Affairs. He was serving out his term exiled to this hell-hole because some supervisor had it in for him. Frank didn't like Deep Creek. The altitude didn't agree with him and it didn't agree with his invalid wife. His sister, who was supposed to keep the school, probably didn't like it much either. The three of them barricaded themselves into the agency, guns hidden in every cranny, and lived on cold flapjacks while they waited for Frank's retirement pay to commence. And then there were the Indians. They were "sullen and insolvent," as Amos Frank put it, and they would not take orders. For the Indians' part, they detested Frank. In early June of 1917, the pot boiled over.

The United States had been at war since 6 April. On 18 May 1917, the Selective Service Act became law. All American males between twenty-one and thirty-one were required to register for the draft. The Indians were not citizens. They did not vote. They were exempt from military service. Still, by law they had to register. There was trouble at the Shoshone reservation at Fort Hall. Letters passed between Anees Tommy in Deep Creek and Indians in Box Elder County, Utah, and at Skull Valley and Fort Hall. In Pocatello, Idaho, a white man called a meeting of prominent Shoshones and in a darkened room of a house in town exhorted the Indians to arm themselves and resist the draft. It was rumored that the Shoshones were taking up a collection to visit Jack Wilson, the Ghost Dance prophet. The war was blazing. German agents lurked everywhere. And out on the flats under Haystack Peak there were twelve young Indians who needed to register for the draft.

Think about it. You are a German agent in the year 1917. You run your finger over the map of the United States, passing up the ammunition dumps of New Jersey, the factories of Massachusetts, the granaries and docks of the Great Lakes. You pass that finger over the great naval storehouses of the West Coast, the vast timberlands of Oregon and Washington and then circle back. There between the Sierra Nevadas and the Rockies, you come to one of the most barren deserts in the world, where the population consists of a few miners, a handful of ranchers and sheepherders, and a straggling band of Indians so unimportant no one bothered to count them for forty years. Your finger stops. You look at those poor, ragged Indians and see them ripe for subversion.

At Deep Creek, Amos Frank called together the Indians and explained the draft law to them through an interpreter. When it came time to register, all of the young men who were eligible suddenly found they had to be in Nevada to shear sheep. The next day a frightened agent for the supression of liquor traffic named Knapp blustered into Ibapah vowing to arrest the ringleaders of the Indian draft resisters. He was detained by a bunch of angry Gosiutes and finally made his way to the little mining town of Gold Hill, where he wired Washington DC, under Superintendent Frank's signature: "Indians at Ibapah in revolt . . . Indians sending messengers over state and Nevada, bringing in other Indians. All have rifles. Would like 40 to 50 soldiers. Will take that many control situation." In Washington, an Indian commissioner inured to such hair-raising wires sent one man.

L. A. Dorrington arrived to investigate the situation at Ibapah and found the Indians posting notices that they were not on the warpath. He discovered that the superintendent was hated, had been hated all along. Dorrington got eight of the Gosiute men to register. The other four were working away from the reservation. As for the Indians who had caused the trouble, it was treason. Dorrington recommended that they be tried.

It was about this time that Doctor Joseph Peck went out to Ibapah to give the Gosiute men who were eligible for registration their physicals.

Peck wasn't too enthusiastic about the whole business of registering the Indians in the first place, but fifty dollars was fifty dollars, so he made the trip. He was newly married, living in a board shanty with a tent lean-to for a bedroom, and trying to scrape together a practice in the little mining town of Gold Hill.

Peck knew Anees Tommy, the leader of the Deep Creek resisters, but he had never gotten along with him. He put it down to professional jealousy, for Anees Tommy was the tribal shaman. In his books and the articles he wrote on his Gold Hill days, Peck describes Anees Tommy howling at the door of sick Indians' wickiups and prophesying death when he wasn't complaining to the "old ladies" of the Indian Rights Society. But Anees Tommy was more than a jealous shaman. He was a traditionalist, and under Peck's jokes and Amos Frank's anger, we see a man fighting for what would be the most evident thing in the world to him, the right to be a Gosiute.

So when Peck got to Ibapah and found none of the young men around, he did not go to Anees Tommy. He went to talk to Tommy's stepfather, Antelope Jake. His description is the last we shall have of this remarkable man.

Jake was over eighty years old and smoked a bag of Bull Durham a day in roll-your-owns. He dressed in an antelopeskin vest with the hair side out. Peck says he welcomed him graciously "for an Indian" and came to the point at once. Jake was worried. He shook his head when Peck tried to explain to him why the boys must go.

"Jake no savvy why Americans have to go so far to fight. How come you know Germans well enough to get mad at them? Who are they and where do they live?"

I explained that we were mad because they sank our ships in the ocean.

Jake replied, "Whose ocean is it anyhow?"

I said it belongs to everybody.

"Well," said Jake, "why not keep our boats at home until the war quiets down? What did the people on the other side have that we needed?"

That one floored me. I fell back on analogies. "Suppose the Paiutes chased your men off the mountains down around Delta when they went there to hunt, how would you feel?"

"But our boys know better than to hunt down there. That is Paiute country and nobody has gone there since Jake was a little boy and we got licked when we did. So we stay home and have no trouble with anybody."

Then Jake asked an interesting question. "What does German look like? You ever see one?" Peck explained to Jake that Germans looked like other white people, and that, because of his name, he was sure that the Ibapah superintendent was of German heritage. At that Jake brightened up:

"You tell white father we kill him for free and any other Germans that come around here too. You go fight your war. Gosiutes will stand behind you and keep Germans from capturing Ibapah valley. . . . We keep boys home. Anybody come here you want killed we do it – Germans, Paiutes, or Indian agents."

Through the summer and into the winter things on the reservation remained at a tense standoff. In mid-January, while the world was addressing the implications of Woodrow Wilson's Fourteen Points, the Gosiutes forced Superintendent Frank to write a letter from them to the Indian commissioner in Washington. Since Amos Frank arrived, they said, the school had been discontinued, and when he hired men to work, they were always whites and Mexicans, never Indians. And what about the Indians killed by whites over the years? Anees Tommy's brother was one of them. "This agent says nothing about it and never tries to help." They had lost land, water, timber to the whites. They insisted that Frank leave by the end of February. Frank appended his own explanation. The Indians who had asked him to write were the same ones who always caused trouble. He recommended that they be punished.

Once more Dorrington returned to Ibapah. He found the Indians united against Amos Frank and bitterly opposed to the draft. A long time ago, Anees Tommy said, the president had told them to put away their arms and fight no more. We told him we would do it, and now you come and want us to fight, but we won't do it.

Dorrington was concerned. Frank was an unbending, illiberal man. He had failed to win the Gosiutes' confidence. But the Indians couldn't be allowed to think they had the power to remove their superintendent. In Salt Lake City Dorrington conferred with the U.S. Attorney and the U.S. Marshal. They issued warrants for Willie Ottogary, Anees Tommy, Al Steel, Jim Straight, and John Syme.

On 20 February 1918, diplomats on three continents were probing and posturing for peace, and Germany was laying plans for a final bloody offensive on the Western Front. Late that same night, in the state of Utah, a detachment of three officers and fifty-one enlisted men from Fort Douglas set out in secret at Gold Hill. Driving cars that Doctor Peck had rounded up for them, they made their way across Clifton Flats and into the Deep Creek Mountains. It was minus twenty degrees Fahrenheit and a foot of new snow had fallen. At dawn the soldiers rushed into the Indian settlement and pulled the men they had come to arrest from their beds. Only Anees Tommy and a couple of other Indians showed any fight. The army confiscated twenty-five rifles and shotguns. Willie Ottogary had been arrested that same day in Tremonton.

That night in Gold Hill there was a dance. The miners' wives had gotten together a meal for the victorious soldiers. There were tubs of coffee and a couple of fiddles to provide the music. Someone had driven over the line to Nevada so out behind the pool hall there were more potent refreshments. Peck remembers seeing the soldiers who had been guarding the Indians leaving the pool hall, their arms around each other, singing "K-K-K-Katy" at the tops of their lungs while their prisoners trailed behind dragging the soldiers' guns and ammunition belts.

The Indian prisoners were taken to Salt Lake City and arraigned. In the photograph the Salt Lake *Tribune* took that winter, the Indians stand around the U.S. Marshal, the wide brims of their hats shadowing their eyes, their clothes the shapeless coarse suitcoats and pants of the frontier. They are short men, dark-faced, unsmiling, with thick trunks and legs. These are the children of those last people to come out of Coyote's water jug, those tough, dust-colored people who some said were bullet-proof.

After three weeks the Gosiutes were released, local whites around Ibapah going their bond. After a while all the charges were dropped for lack of evidence. By May, Amos Frank had succeeded in having Anees Tommy and his family removed from the reservation. The Gosiute war was over, and he had his victory. Frank wondered, though, whether Agent Knapp, deputy special officer for the suppression of the liquor traffic, hadn't really been a German spy, inciting the Indians the way he had.

"Every man," anthropologist Clifford Geertz writes, "has a right to create his own savage for his own purposes." The Dust People had no need to create savages in order to see themselves reflected against the world, in order to define themselves and know who they were. The Dust People had no need to create savages, because they had us.

The seeds of knowledge are within us like fire in flint.
Descartes

Now they were in the desert where desire was tested. Out in the sand whirl-winds twisted and danced. High clouds floated in the serene blue sky, mocking them. Everything was unreal. Coyote twitched. It meant some-one was thinking about him.

The water in their jugs was gone. They bribed Coyote with the marrow bones that were all they had left from their hunt. When Coyote got back they all were dead. He went from one to the other and revived them with the water, and when they were alive again he jumped up and fell upon the pile of marrow bones, but his boys had sucked all the marrow out and left the bones hard and dry, and they clattered emptily together. Then all the boys laughed at Coyote, slapped their legs and yipped. He fell into the dust and moaned. They were still a long way from the land of fire.

At last they arrived at a green land on the other side of the Dusty Path. It was the land of fire. The people with fire looked at Coyote cagily. They wanted to know what Coyote and his friends were doing in their land. "Oh," Coyote replied, "we're just going around visiting other camps, the way we always do." He took a couple of pieces of wood from the thong around his waist. "What would we do with fire anyway," he said, "since we already have fire-drills?"

Coyote and his people had crossed the Dusty Path to a strange land. Ev-erything was backwards there. Everything was upside-down. It was a world on the other side of hospitality where the gift of fire was hoarded. Who were these people who kept the fire? Were they people at all? Coyote's children were a race who didn't know much about owning things. A man might own a medicine vision, a gambling song, or an eagle's nest. He might own a bow, or a woman might own a basket. No one owned the groves of pine nuts or the seeds and roots they used for food, or the meat that the lucky hunter shared with everyone. No one should own the secret of fire.

Do not speak openly of the dead. To name them, to even think or dream them, is dangerous. Jealous and lonely in their cold land, they are always ready to steal the breath of the living, to trick them into joining them. They are always fretful, always suspicious, and they do not give up their secrets gladly.

36

Night fell, and Coyote's people came into the camp. And what they did then, suspicious hosts and cunning guests, is what hosts and guests always do: they sat down to gamble. It was the only communication the people who keep the fire would allow. There, on the other side of the Dusty Path, in that land at the end of desire, it was the only vice.

The game they played was a simple one. Separated by the fire, the hosts and guests became hiders and guessers. Side by side two hiders manipulated the bones behind a blanket, one pair of bones wrapped, the other pair plain; they moved them back and forth with many subtle gestures between their hands. And while they gambled, they sang. They taunted the guessers, mocked their skill. They called upon the little animals to help them, the mice and squirrels who knew how to hide things in the earth.

Left hand right hand left hand right hand . . .

Swaying back and forth, while their fellows drummed upon a plank, the Ghosts hid the bones. It was a game so simple its only meaning was made possible by human emotion, human story, human symbol. There were only four possibilities: both naked bones would be in the hiders' left hands, both in their right, or one in each. In the dead mind of a machine, knowing only the language of number, it is a sort of nongame; in the living minds of human beings and the memories of Ghosts, it was a game of complexity and depth, of feints and parries, of magic and cunning, luck and skill. For every bet advanced was a little life wagered, every bet lost was a little death.

So, in the mythworld, the gamblers played into a kind of trance. Divided by the blanket, they could not see beyond the game itself, beyond the firelight which mesmerized them so that only the moving hands of their opponents had meaning and everything beyond was shadow. In the dark silence beyond the game, those gestures and shouts, those mimetic cries, were meaningless, were the gesticulations of madmen. The unspoken meaning of the moment was terrible: caught up by the game, the deadly wish of the contestants was *that the night would never end.*

Without division, light from dark, nature from culture, woman from man, would speech be possible? Would human life itself be possible? To guess a secret, or to keep one, is to own power. The handgame was a way of separating guessers from hiders, winners from losers, the living from the dead. And so it is a version of the story embedded in the story itself. But the game always goes too far. Caught in its powerful rhythms, in the rise and fall of its emotions, in its hypnotic power, the contenders fall into a kind of sleep.

Ha! With a shout, the blanket is dropped. The hiders sit with their arms crossed over their chests. And now the chief guesser gets to work. With many sly, probing feints he begins to point – then pulls back, bluffs, and stutters – while suggestions, possibilities, convictions come at him from all sides. Then with the ritual cry he points, and the guess is made.

But fire can never be won. It must be exterior to the game, beyond skill or luck, in a territory that only a terrible foolishness can penetrate. Overvalued, distended in its cruel logic, the game does not intensify reality, it swallows it. Coyote knows that fire can never be won, it must be seized. For consciousness is the last audacity. It is a theft that liberates fire from sleep, that breaks the iron laws of games. So while the others gamble, Coyote dances. Caught in the narcotic of play, the winning and losing, no one will notice him as he dances between the living and the dead.

lefthandrighthandlefthandrighthand . . .

A couple of toothless hags are watching the flames. Sunk into a sort of senile second virginity, they are beyond both pollution and desire. They are beyond childbearing. They are beyond gambling. What's left for them but to stir the mush pot and guard the fire? Fire, blood, semen – they are magical substances, filled with potency, capable of great damage if one doesn't guard against pollution around them. The hunter is continent before the hunt, a prudent person is careful to observe the taboos of menstruation, careful around the fire. Man is to woman as the fire-drill is to the hearth, as the arrow is to the wound. The old hags do not notice how close Coyote dances to the flames.

lefthandrighthandlefthandrighthand . . .

The old women guarding the fire begin to doze. Coyote is a clown, he is a fucker. No one will notice him now . . .

lefthandrighthandlefthandrighthand . . .

Coyote dances closer and closer to the fire. His hair is full of cedar shreds. His hair is full of tinder robbed from Rat's hidden nest. The smoke from the fire rises crazily from its heart, twisting and turning, no one knows where. Who can tell where fire will go, once it starts? Who can tell where it will run? Who can put it out? *Pow!* the power squirts through

38

Coyote's hands. He is juggling it. He is trying to hold it. He can hold it even if his hands explode. Pow! He is juggling the fire in his hands, laughing madly while he dances, while the gamblers make their bets . . .

..

Now he runs! He's danced so close to the flames that his headdress has caught fire! Too late do the old women cry out. Too late do the Ghosts rise from the trance of the game. He runs.

Now, one after another, Coyote's people pass on the fire in a desperate relay race against the pursuing Ghosts. As the birds had risen into the sky one by one, trying to catch sight of the land of fire in the opening of the tale, now the creatures of the mythtime race along the ground, race back across the Dusty Path to their homes at its close, thieves of fire.

The Ghosts send rain to drench the precious seed of fire; still the animals race on, passing the secret coal from one to the other. The fire singes Jackrabbit under the puff of hair where he has hidden it, it scorches Sage Hen's breast. The ghosts run on in pursuit, and their land darkens behind them. At last Rat hides the last spark deep in his tindery nest, and fire is saved. Coyote revives the creatures the Ghosts have killed with a magic cane.

Gibbering and sighing, the Ghosts retreat to their cold and fireless land. Fire is the emblem of consciousness. It must belong to one world or the other. It cannot be shared by living and dead. Henceforth it is Coyote's children who will have the gift of fire. Flickering, dying, almost extinct, it has been hidden in the fur and feathers of the creatures who are humankind's fellows, and now lies latent in the hearth of the fire-drill, only waiting to be spun out, blown up into full being with the merest breath. Henceforth, fire will be useful. It is fire that makes us human, after all. Fire around which we sit to gamble or tell stories such as this, fire that warms the skin, that lights the dangerous world of night and purifies the sweat lodge. It is to fire that we pray after a night of bad dreams, fire that heats the natal bed and purges a woman after childbirth, it is fire that is the beginning of agriculture, as fields are burned off to accept the precious seed. It is fire, at the end, that separates the land of the living from that of the dead, fire that burns the wickiup out of which the corpse is dragged and that burns the possessions his jealous ghost had once used on earth – the bows, the baskets, the blankets, the ornaments, the Mexican saddle, the Ford car – all those things for which one might have gambled. And finally, it is fire that separates us irrevocably from nature. For, having helped Coyote steal the fire by hiding it in their fur and feathers, Rat, Jackrabbit, Sage

Hen now become Coyote's meat; roasted over the coals, they are transformed from his brothers and sisters to his food. For having separated itself from the world of the dead by his theft of fire, humanity can only complete its quest for consciousness by its separation from its fellow animals by the invention of cooking.

..

Sage Hen, who once saved the fire, roasts on the spit, and our father Coyote eats with the grease dribbling down his chin and the savor of his cooking friend in his nostrils. Coyote doesn't writhe chained to his rock, pecked at by the eagle of the gods like that poor Greek who once, long ago, may have been Coyote too. Prometheus brought men fire and placed in them blind hopes. But no Shoshonean ever aspired to be a deathless god, or to wish for a world any better than the one he or she knew. The world Coyote made with his tricks and his mistakes is full enough. Let the Ghosts gnaw their fleshless lips in their cold, jealous land. Fireless, deathless, their green land is only a fiction, a parody of the land of the living, as its narcotic game is a parody of life. No one should gamble for fire.

10   THE END OF THE MYTHTIME

The voices of the animals, who once talked like humans, are gone: Wolf's voice, Cottontail's, voice, Coyote the trickster's voice, with its comical terminal stutter – all of them are gone. Some of the old stories are still told, but much of the texture of their telling has been lost with the world that made them. The gestures, the voices of the men and women who told the tales around the winter fires when there was no other language in the world but their own are finished. Bare words remain, where once the mythtime was, when the animals spoke like people, each with its own voice, its own song, its magic dance.

The mythical world of the Shoshoneans, like that of the Europeans, began in a utopia, a kind of Eden beyond the far border of their desert land, where hunting was without toil and death was unknown. Shamans who went down the Dusty Path to call back the lost soul of some boy or girl saw the place: verdant, abundant. A soul might tarry on the way to that green land to eat chokecherries and the shaman would bring it back to a world that was often harsh, bitter, but, after all, not a dream. For the European, if utopia lay at the beginning of the world, it also lay at its end. It existed in

40

the eternal perfection of a Christian Heaven or, later on, in those maps of some future ideal society sketched out by dreamers and reformers and lunatics: between those two points, those shining places — and this is the source of the melancholy and despair of so much European literature — there was only a terrible nostalgia. For the Shoshoneans there was no such utopia at the end of time. The blandishments of the other world, that green land beyond the Dusty Path, were, like those chokecherries reflected in the stream that Coyote was always trying to get, an illusion. It is this world that is our true home.

..

So, much of the old culture of the Shoshoneans is gone, absorbed by a world of pickup trucks and television, of government and tribal agencies and tape decks and computer files. Often only traces are left, in a story, a song, a formula, a ceremony, a dance. The Dust People — the Gosiutes — still remain. They live now on two reservations in the Utah desert. They farm, raise some cattle, go off to Elko or Reno or Salt Lake to find work. The desert is scabbed over by the refuse of mines that white men have dug into the earth for silver and gold and for those exotic minerals the uses of which are so rarefied that few but specialists know them. The Indians replaced what they took from the earth, left a bead, a charm, a bit of tobacco. The miners and engineers have only taken. For the Indian, the desert was rich, a place full of story and sustenance. For the white man any land barren of material wealth is empty, a place to store nerve gas and detonate weapons, to bury nuclear waste. During World War II, in a huddle of makeshift buildings a few miles west of the place where Coyote had tamed the women with vaginal teeth and fathered humanity, were assembled the bombs that would destroy Hiroshima and Nagasaki.

In their own stubborn way, the Gosiutes, those last children of Coyote to climb out of the water bottle, are still fighting for their lives, still burdened by the imposition of an alien culture that began to affect them before they had even seen the first white face, when the Spanish settlement of Santa Fe set the Utes to stealing Gosiute women and children to sell as slaves. During the MX crisis of the late 1970s and early 1980s the Gosiutes joined a confederation of other Great Basin tribes to oppose the missile system on their lands. Like many tribes and bands, the Gosiutes have been split between traditionalists and those who see their only chance for betterment in making some accommodation with white men and white ways. As I write this passage, the Skull Valley branch of the tribe was studying the feasibility of storing spent fuel rods from nuclear power plants on their lands under a government grant. These people, who always demanded so little from their austere environment, now contemplate their survival as the toxic dumping ground of a society that cannot live except by consuming more than it can replace.

Still, if many of the old Shoshonean ways have disappeared, an essential thing remains: that view that teaches us that we need not see the world as a place tragically flawed, as a utopia forever lost. That view that tells us that we still have left to us all the tools our father Coyote gave us: courage and cunning – as well as cowardice and bluff; ingenuity – as well as appetite and foolishness; and above all, our great ancestor's laughter. These are the tools we need to continue our great project, which is, when all is said and done, the survival of human consciousness in a world which becomes, it often seems, increasingly more hostile to the people who invented it.

Tongues of Fire,
Tongues of Gold

I

In the twenty-sixth canto of Dante's *Inferno* we come to the tortured soul of Ulysses, envisioned as a gigantic tongue of flame that trembles and swells as it tells the story of the hero's last voyage. The punishment is appropriate: through his eloquence, Ulysses has transgressed a linguistic boundary, the boundary that sets apart the imaginary world. Grown old, with the last of those men who had not deserted him, Ulysses sails out beyond the Pillars of Hercules into an unknown sea, and there addresses his reluctant crew:

> 'Brothers,' I said, 'who through a hundred thousand
> perils have made your way to reach the West,
> during this so brief vigil of our senses
> That is still reserved for us, do not deny
> yourself experience of what there is beyond,
> behind the sun, in the world they call unpeopled.
>
> 'Consider what you came from: you are Greeks!
> you were not born to live like mindless brutes
> but to follow paths of excellence and knowledge.'

This brief speech is enough: the crew sails on.

43

> Five times we saw the splendor of the moon
> grow full and five times wane away again. . . .
> When there appeared a mountain shape, darkened
> by distance, that arose to endless heights.

In Dante's mind the geography that took Ulysses beyond the Pillars of Hercules and out into the western ocean was real enough, and the hero's transgression was clear, for the mountain rising out of the western sea on the unknown, watery hemisphere, was Mount Purgatory. In Dante, Purgatory (for all his belief in its literal dimension) is a thing of the mind and such sights are not meant for the living: a great whirlpool rises from the ocean and sucks Ulysses' ship under, and now the Greek burns for eternity in the eighth *bolgia,* as a giver of false counsel.

Not two centuries after Dante completed his great poem, another mariner much given to visions and prophecies became convinced that he had come to the Holy Mountain. It rose not as a terrific, lone peak, as Dante had believed, but was a gentle swelling on the orb of the earth, like the stem end of a pear, or a woman's nipple. A new man, steeped in the sciences of the Renaissance and the drive for worldly conquest, half-inhabited by the fables of the Middle Ages, Columbus had sailed beyond the Pillars of Hercules and found, near the outlet of the Orinoco, the slope of Paradise. The language of this discovery is significant: located now in a geography of real coasts and tides and plottable meridians, Paradise becomes something to be touched and consumed. And thus it happens that the New World is born in a monumental confusion between literature and geography.

2

Eu = Good. Topos = Place. The Good Place. Ou = No. Topos = Place. No Place. Nowhere. There, at the edge of culture, balanced on the unsteady margin between the two possibilities of a Greek pun, utopia is the place that can never be attained, only imagined. Unlike Heaven (or, for that matter, Hell) it is a version of the world whose very utility is its insubstantiality. Since Sumerian Dilmun, since Homer's Isles of the Blessed, and Plato's Atlantis, since Eden, the dream has fastened on the Western mind.

In Montaigne's celebrated essay of 1578–80 "Of Cannibals," the dream is located in the fastness of Brazil. From the talk of one of his servants who had visited the New World, and through the writings of other travelers, Montaigne examines the slanders against the cannibals of what he calls

Antarctic France and finds them baseless. Trying both by internal logic and by analogy to understand this strange people, he even goes so far as to sample for himself the Brazilians' cassava root cake. It is a remarkable passage. Here the man of the Renaissance, not content to learn by hearsay or the testimony of the ancients, does something unthinkable: he eats the cannibals' bread.

"I have tried it; it tastes sweet and a little flat."

But Montaigne goes still further, and uses the differences between the French and the cannibals to interrogate the meaning of culture itself. For, when all is said and done, Montaigne is not really interested in cannibals. He is interested in Frenchmen. The New World serves as a kind of intellectual lever, a way of distancing himself from the Old World in order to see it whole, and in so doing, to judge it:

This is a nation, I should say to Plato, in which there is no sort of traffic, no knowledge of letters, no science of numbers, no name for a magistrate or for political superiority, no custom of servitude, no riches or poverty, no contracts, no successions, no partitions, no occupations but leisure ones, no care for any but common kinship, no clothes, no agriculture, no metal, no use of wine or wheat. The very words that signify lying, treachery, dissimulation, avarice, envy, belittling, pardon – unheard of. How far from this perfection would he find the republic that he imagined.

Well before the publication of Montaigne's essay on cannibals Thomas More had located his Utopia (1517), from whence the general term for all such projects of the mind would come, in a New World then scarcely known to Europeans. Thus, from the first, utopias are truly nowheres; they are constructs of the mind set in a West that is magical, that exists not in itself but as a sort of solvent to the old ideas and the limits of history. For Europe is always offstage in these works: it is America that is the specter. And so it is that Shakespeare, in *The Tempest*, restores Montaigne's America to its true location, which is the geography of the European mind. Put into the mouth of the old counselor Gonzalo, and translated into the blank verse of the Elizabethan stage, Montaigne's speech becomes airy, naive, wishful. Indeed, what *The Tempest* is about is language itself. It is Prospero's speech that holds his island together, that is its true government. The magic of language – always fragile, apt at any moment to turn inward, to annul or contradict itself – is the thin web that suspends world, audience,

TONGUES OF FIRE, TONGUES OF GOLD 45

history, and time. It is the spell of language that keeps this imagined island from disintegrating into the fragmented, horrible world of Caliban's original inarticulate grunts and groans. Caliban. The word itself is an anagram of Cannibal—as if backwards lies unimaginable savagery. And forward, of course, lies the innocent Miranda's brave new world.

3

In the year 1537 there came to the Spanish court a nobleman who had late been in the New World. This man, Álvar Núñez Cabeza de Vaca, had a remarkable adventure to relate. He had gone out in 1528 as treasurer to the ill-fated Narváez expedition to Florida. He, with two other Spaniards, and Esteban, the North African slave of one of these other adventurers, were the only survivors known of that company of 400 men who had set out from Cuba to conquer the unknown lands to the north. (Later, De Soto would come upon another survivor of the expedition living among the Indians in Florida.)

For eight years Cabeza de Vaca had been a sojourner on this broad continent of North America. He had been shipwrecked and had heard of companions driven to cannibalism, of others drowning in flooded rivers, dying one by one of starvation, killed by the savages that peopled this godless land. Like the other Spaniards of the company, he had come to America for gold and slaves; but he had become a slave himself and to the very people he had set out to conquer. He had grubbed for roots in the canebrakes and in the water, his fingers so raw that they bled if a straw touched them. And he had become, although he did not then know it, one of the first Europeans to cross the North American continent.

The land he found himself in was a land of dreams. Of narcotic mesquite beans, peyote, the black drink. Of demons such as the one whose name he translated as Mala Cosa, who ripped the entrails from the Indians, severed their limbs, and by magic stuck them back together again. In this hallucinatory world Cabeza de Vaca had survived by trading on his Otherness. He had become, with the three sharers of his adventure, first a healer and then, by himself, a merchant, trafficking in seashells and mesquite beans, bartering them for skins, red ochre face paint, hard canes for arrows, flint for arrowheads, sinews and cement and deer-hair tassels. "This occupation suited me," he wrote. "I could travel where I wished, was not obliged to work, and was not a slave. Wherever I went, the Indians treated me honorably and gave me food, because they liked my commodities."

Both merchants and shamans carry passports between two worlds. Located on the far margins of culture by virtue of who they are – the stranger, the *berdache,* the mentally ill – they are apt mediators between the world of the spirit and that of humankind, between tribes often hostile to one another, people who speak in different tongues. So when at last Cabeza de Vaca and the other castaways were able to make their way west, it was as proto-merchants and shamans that they went. Surrounding them was a great train of Indians, for the strangers had achieved the reputation of being great healers and prophets. Their trail through the Indian towns of what are now Texas and northern Mexico, and into the Mexican state of Sonora, became a triumphal progress, accompanied by miraculous cures and prophecies and massive transfers of goods between tribes who had often been at war – a progress that anticipated, perhaps, the wholesale conversions of Indians to Christianity that would begin later on, for these naked once-conquistadors had become gods on their journey to where the sun sets. "They [the Indians] were convinced that we came from Heaven. (Anything that is new to them or beyond their comprehension is explained as coming from Heaven.)"

Stripped of his honors, of his history, remote from his God, Cabeza de Vaca had experienced that profound sense of losing the boundaries of his soul that may be the heart of mystical experience. His very body had ceased to enclose him. Like the Indians, he was naked, twice a year shedding his skin as would a snake.

Language too, became permeable, magical, in this mystical trek: "We passed from one strange tongue to another, but God our Lord always enabled each new people to understand us and we them. You would have thought, from the questions and answers in signs, that they spoke our language and we theirs."

..

Crossing the Yaqui River in late January of 1536, the castaways came across the vanguard of the Christian world: a band of slavers. When the whites saw Cabeza de Vaca, naked, accompanied by the Moor Esteban and eleven Indians, they were dumbfounded: they did not hail him, but could only stand staring. Cabeza de Vaca himself was like a man who had forgotten a language he had spoken a long time ago. As if it were rusty with disuse, he at last found his voice and asked the soldiers to take him to their captain. At Compostella the Royal Governor received the lost men and outfitted them from his own wardrobe. But it was some time before Cabeza de Vaca could stand to wear any clothes, or sleep anyplace but the bare floor. The Indian world had become a part of him in a profound way. Indeed, Álvar Núñez Cabeza de Vaca had become the first American. For to be an American is not a geographical distinction but a mental one. It is to be caught between two worlds, the old and the new, to be a part of neither and of both. Only a few lost Europeans and Cortez's Indian translator and mistress, La Malinche, before him could tell us what that strange and precarious identity was like, but they do not speak.

Back in Spain, Cabeza de Vaca told, in fact, two stories. The one was rendered in his studied silence, which became a vessel into which his hearers poured their hopes and dreams and which sent De Soto to disaster and helped procure for Cabeza de Vaca an appointment as *adelantado* of the provinces of the Rio de la Plata, and more adventures and trials. The other was told in the sober pages of the *Relación* he took with him to Spain. In the *Relación* Cabeza de Vaca wrote of a journey through a land of hunger, where only his wits and his faith kept him from disaster. The austere description of the land, its peoples, and their customs, and its writer's incessant manipulation of appearance and reality to provide a new identity in a new land, put the *Relación* halfway between those travelers' tales the exploration of the Americas would begin to produce and – it would be twelve years before the publication of *Lazarillo de Tormes,* the first of its genre – the picaresque. In his person, Cabeza de Vaca had united the shaman of the Indian to the *picaro* of Spain. Half Prospero, half rogue, this figure is the glue that patches up the cracks in utopia, the mediator between reality and utopia's fatally flawed schemes of hope.

4

Since the Middle Ages there had been, on the Iberian peninsula, a legend of six bishops and an archbishop who, fleeing the Moors with their people, had sailed westward into the Sea of Darkness and, beyond the farthest lands known to Europeans, had founded seven cities on an island called Antillia.

The Island of the Seven Cities was the product of the wish of a dying Christian kingdom; it had come out of the ancient traditions of the Celtic and Greco-Roman world, stories of those islands toward which the soul journeys after death. On Renaissance maps the Island of Antillia moved from latitude to latitude in the vast unknown of the Atlantic, keeping company with islands real and imagined, the Canaries, the Cape Verdes, St. Brendan's Isle, the mystical Island of Brazil. In 1492, the year of Columbus's landfall in the New World, Martin Dehaim's planisphere showed Antillia west of the Cape Verdes. Columbus, who knew Dehaim, may have hoped to use it as a stepping-stone to Cipangu.

With the conquest of Mexico, the legends of the Seven Cities blended with those of the Indian nations that the Spaniards subjected, stories of the Nahua's origins in Aztlan, of seven caves. The Indians were not slow to feed this hunger the Spaniards had for such tales. It was a way, after all, of sending these bearded, gold-maddened men off to the next chain of hills.

Always for the conquistadors the New World hovers in this place where fiction and desire meet, the one blazing up in the other. For though it was America, the world the Spanish conquerors not infrequently found themselves wandering through was that of their own fantastic literature. It was the books that they brought to the New World by the galleon-ful that populated their imaginations with dreams of jewel-studded cities and magic enchantments and, hard by the Terrestrial Paradise, a golden island peopled with Amazons.

Know that on the right hand of the Indies there is an island called California, very close to the side of the Terrestrial Paradise; and it was peopled by black women, without any man among them, for they lived in the fashion of Amazons. They were of strong and hardy bodies, of ardent courage and great force. Their island was the strongest in all the world, with its steep cliffs and rocky shores. Their arms were all of gold, and so was the harness of the wild beasts which they tamed to ride; for in the whole island there was no metal but gold.

It was as if, in the twilight of a dying chivalry, the Spaniards were overcome with an overwhelming nostalgia for a mythic past. There, at the beginning of the modern age, they saw the New World through the eyes of their own Amadis of Gaul and Palmerin and Esplandian and the bright fictions that called them up. The bloody deeds and material ambitions of the reconquest had been recast in the chivalric gestures of a courtly dance, of knightly battles with giants and creatures pasted together out of the shreds of classical and Arthurian mythologies, of visits to strange islands, invisible, or floating in the air, of lands inhabited by man-eating Elestrigons and the dog-faced Cenofales Barbacans, of horrific battles for an imaginery Constantinople. Now, underneath the mythological embroideries of this failed literature was something darker still, for such fictions veiled the more terrible deeds the conquistadors had yet to do in the New World. About to embark on the conquest of Mexico, Cortez prayed that God would give him and his company the same good fortune in fighting that he gave the Paladin Roland. When Cortez's men first beheld Tenochtitlán they compared it to the enchanted things related by Amadis of Gaul, and some of the soldiers asked if what they saw were not a dream. The margins of the Spaniards' fantastic books came to be annotated by the hanged and decapitated and ravaged bodies of the native peoples of the New World. We have a disease, Cortez told the Aztecs, that can only be cured by gold. And as in so many things, the conquistador proved right. For Cortez possessed in a large measure that great gift for conquest: the ability to see clearly the hard rules of its business, while at the same time projecting them into the realms of mythologized wish. So Cortez, like the rest of the Spaniards, made his way through the New World, a wide-awake man walking in a dream.

For the gold hunger itself was wrapped in dreams. And like a dream, its prize kept eluding the conquistadors. It was as if the fabulous treasures of Mexico and Peru were only goads to failure, a kind of intermittent reinforcement of the lust for gold. The English traveler Henry Hawks inadvertently caught the truth of it.

The Spanyards have notice of seven cities which old men of the Indians shew them should lie towards the Northwest from Mexico. They have used and use dayly much dilligence in seeking of them, but they cannot find any one of them. They say that the witchcraft of the Indians is such, that when they come by these townes they cast a mist upon them, so that they cannot see them.

The witchcraft that covered the Seven Cities in mist was not in the powers of the Indians, after all, but in the minds of those who sought them.

On the east coast of Mexico an Indian told Nuño de Guzman of an expedition he and his father had made into the northern interior, carrying fine feathers for ornaments, which they traded for gold and silver. In that land he encountered seven rich and populous cities, with streets of silver workers. Because the Spaniards desired them (as they desired a New World peopled by Amazons, washed with streams of gold) the Seven Golden Cities were there. And the name Cíbola, as the cities soon came to be called, would become a kind of ghostly Signifier floating before the Spaniards from one huddled Indian village to the next like a flag.

Because Esteban, or Estevánico as he is sometimes called, could not write, Fray Marcos of Nice, the Franciscan that the Viceroy Mendoza had chosen to reconnoiter the unknown lands to the north, devised with the Moor a system of signs to be used as Esteban hurried ahead across the wasteland before him.

I agreed with him that if he had any news of a populous, rich and important country he should not continue further but should return in person or send me Indians with a certain signal which we arranged, namely, that if it were something of medium importance, he should send me a white cross of a hand's breadth, if it were something of great importance, he should send me one of two hands' breadth, while if it were bigger and better than New Spain, he should send me a great cross.

When Cabeza de Vaca walked out of the dream land of the north, he brought with him stories of turquoises and stones he thought to be emeralds that had come from a town of great houses of which the Indians had told him. And he had brought a magical rattle that had served his party well in their journey to the west. Now Esteban marched north, bearing the gourd rattle into the land of the pagans before him. Free in the space between two signs, the cross behind him, the rattle before, Esteban, the man from Azamor, the man who was still a slave, tasted for the short days remaining to him the power to reinvent himself.

Unconstrained by the limitations of the written page, in Esteban's hands the mythological sign bloomed: four days after he left Fray Marcos, the Moor sent an Indian back to the priest with a cross as big as a man. The Indian told Fray Marcos that Esteban was entering a country of seven great cities, where the doorways of the houses were studded with turquoise stones. The name of the first city was called by the Indians Cíbola.

Dressed in the guise of the southwestern native shaman, with plumes on his feet and arms and wearing on his body rattles and bells, Esteban entered the city of Cíbola with his harem of Indian girls and packs full of extorted wealth, only to be betrayed by the sacred rattle. For in the end, the magic signs failed Esteban. Or he failed them. By its markings the people of Cíbola recognized the magical rattle as belonging to a people with whom they were bitterly at odds, and Esteban was isolated in the pueblo, interrogated, and finally killed. Arguing for his life, Esteban had made his skin itself a sign, for he told the elders of Zuni that white men would follow him. Faced with the unknown, the elders reasoned better than the Spaniards:

for why would these powerful white men of whom the strange, bearded shaman spoke send a black man before them? Interrogation, then execution, was the fate meted out in Zuni to the witch.

As for Fray Marcos, he had only glimpsed the pueblo in the distance and it seemed in that light to be a great city. What the priest wrote in his report to his Father Provincial was the truth. He had noted carefully what he had seen, without exaggeration, penetrating the Indian languages with a remarkable fidelity (except that once he had imagined they told him of a fabulous one-horned beast, such as one found in the forbidden books of romance, garbling their description of a buffalo). But he told what he had heard the Indians say as well. Like Cabeza de Vaca, who had stirred speculation by his strategic silences in Spain, the friar's language split in two: there was the "truth" of the written language for his superiors, to be sure, but what about the tales that the priest had let drop while being shaved? Were there two truths, one for the sober pages of a report, the other for the barber's chair? Somehow the story got out about towns with high walls and gates, and women with strings of golden beads and men with belts of gold, and streets of silversmiths and sheep and cows and partridges and iron forges. In Mexico City men were trading for licenses allowing them to go to Cíbola as soldiers, and it was as if the country would become depopulated by those who wished to go.

6

When they got to Cíbola they found not the fabled cities of romance, only the rough stone houses of an Indian pueblo, "a little, unattractive village, looking as if it had been crumpled all up together." Coronado had come with his army. He had stopped before the walls of the pueblo and ordered the *requerimiento* read to the uncomprehending Indians as was legal and fit. His solders broke through the lines of sacred cornmeal by which the Zunis had thought to contain them, and then Coronado defeated the Indians. But the Seven Cities yielded no gold, no emeralds, only maize, pumpkins, cotton cloths. Finding no treasures, Coronado could only taste the tortillas and report that they were very good. Fearing for Fray Marcos's life – for he had accompanied the expedition and now had to face the disappointment of men who had followed his tales, real or supposed, to this miserable village of rock and mud – Coronado sent the priest back to Sonora and pushed on.

Somewhere east of Cíbola, at a place called Cicuye (perhaps the Pecos ruins) the Spaniards came across a plausible rogue they called, because of his looks, the Turk. The Turk was a slave, a Wichita Indian who told them of a place to the east he called Quivira, and he spun them a tale of that land that set them afire. In Quivira, the Turk said, there was a river two leagues wide in which there were fishes as big as horses, and large numbers of big canoes with sails and twenty rowers on a side. And the lords of the Indians sat on the poops of the canoes under awnings, and on the prow they had a great golden eagle. And the lord of that country took his afternoon nap under a great tree on which were hung a great number of little gold bells which put him to sleep as they swung in the air. In Quivira the houses were made of stone. Even the household vessels were made of silver and gold. The Spaniards, naturally, believed the Turk.

They came to a level land that in later times would be called the Staked Plain. The land was so flat and smooth it was as if a man should imagine himself standing in a three-pint measure and could see nothing but the sky at the edge. Here were only the buffalo, endless, drove on drove. A hailstorm burst upon the men, shattering everything breakable in their camp. The whirlwind that accompanied it carried away tents, coverings, even some of the horses. In the dawn there were only the plains again. Now they began to suffer pitiably from thirst. They had no more maize to eat, only buffalo.

They happened upon a tribe of Indians, perhaps the Utes, following the buffalo with their dogs and travoises. They knew Quivira, but it was a poor country, with little corn. The buildings were not stone, but straw and skins. The Spaniards put the Turk in chains and marched on. On Ascension Day, 1541, Coronado split his company; he, with the two Indian slaves and twenty-nine horsemen, set off to the east.

For fifteen days the rest of the company remained where Coronado left them. Waiting for their general, the army began to succumb to the hysteria that had always been just below the surface since they arrived on the plains. Hunters went off after buffalo, didn't return, were lost on the prairie. For days the lost men wandered about the country as if they were mad, not knowing how to get back where they started from. Those who returned said all they had seen in the days of their wandering were sky and the cows. Every night they took account of who was missing, fired guns and blew trumpets and beat drums and built great fires. In their rage and despair the soldiers fell to slaughtering the buffalo indiscriminately, killing perhaps 500 bulls in a fortnight. Then they left the plains heaped with carcasses and set off for the pueblos to the west. If there was no gold, their desire had no meaning. On the trail to the east, Coronado, thinking he was nearing Quivira, sat down to write a letter to its prince. Still under the enchantment of the tales of the Turk, he imagined this prince to be a Christian (perhaps a survivor of the wrecked fleet of Narváez?), some kind of Prester John in the fastness of America.

On 21 August, Coronado found Quivira in the center of Kansas. Bits of iron pyrites and a few pieces of copper were the only metals he could discover. The people were savages, living in round huts and tipis. They planted a little corn, dressed in skins, followed the buffalo, ate their meat raw. One night the Spaniards slipped a garrote around the Turk's neck and choked off his tales for good. He had been lying all the time, trying to lead them off into the plains where the horses would die and the Spaniards would be helpless. Twenty-five days later Coronado set out to rejoin his army. He had found only good soil, plums, grapes, mulberries. At the end of his trail he left a wooden cross with the following words cut into it: "Francisco Vásquez de Coronado, leader of a campaign, came to this place." But the cross marked only an arbitrary point on a land without borders. Quivira wasn't even a spot on a map; it was the hunting grounds of a tribe, rootless, savage, wandering in skins and living in skin houses, following the great herds of buffalo, knowing nothing of gold.

Lies. Lies, all of it. The rich land of Floridian Apalachen, bejeweled Cíbola, golden Quivira. The Spaniards' dreams dilated in the gap between the languages they knew and those they did not. Those signs, expressions, pantomimes where the modern world, with its insatiable demand for gold and power, thought to reach the aboriginal world could only be misread, willfully, brutally. At Zuni the Spaniards might have indeed found a version of Utopia, had they only been able to see it. Caught in a round of ritual and magic, the pueblo was an Amerindian version of the golden theocracy of the Seven Cities of Antillia. In the careful social balance of Zuni and the other pueblos the Spaniards might have discovered something analogous to the classical Golden Age. Indeed, when Coronado came to the pueblos, he had been unable to find a chief's house taller than the others. But the Spaniards who lived among these graceful people for two winters, who watched the women with their hair "gathered about the ears like little wheels" going to and fro in the plaza, and witnessed the ceremonies of the men's kachina cults, saw nothing of this. Only once, for a moment, in Castañeda's account, do we glimpse the world the Spaniards might have found: in front of a room in a pueblo a man sits playing on a flute; the women are kneeling over the stone trough inside, grinding corn to the rhythm of the tune. They are singing in unison. It is only a glimpse, nothing more. The door Castañeda has opened to the Indian world shuts and is never opened again. For the people of the pueblos were everything their conquerors were not. The Spaniards had come to the New World, as one of them once put it, "to serve God and his Majesty, to give light to those who were in darkness and to grow rich as all men desire to do." In Zuni and the other Indian towns, the Spaniards found a people who submerged individuality in the group, whose wealth was measured in spiritual power. Delicately balancing the competing worlds of men and women and diverting aggression through complex social and religious negotiations, obsessive in their ceremonialism as any saint planning a new monastic order, or Fourierist chartering a utopian phalanx, the Indians of the pueblos had created a world in which the sterner virtues, as one anthropologist termed them — initiative, ambition, and uncompromising sense of honor and justice, intense personal loyalties — were only to be deplored. It would be hard to find a race more unlike the conquistadors of 1540.

The beautiful fictions that had inspired these European adventurers overthrown, what was left was only a poignant sense of loss. Castañeda, thinking years later of the old soldiers of the Coronado expedition, which he so movingly chronicled, wrote, "Since they came back from the country which they conquered and abandoned, time has given them a chance to understand the direction and locality in which they were, and the borders of the good country they had in their hands, and their hearts weep for having lost so favorable an opportunity."

..

So they go off, the conquistadors, following one lie after another into the great, featureless prairie, and every disappointment stiffens their willingness to believe in what they seek. But when they get to that fabled place, which is truly nowhere (because it is inside them), they kill the Turk. His function has consumed itself; there are no more lies left to tell. Poor Turk! What, after all, had he done but spin them a tale out of Amadis of Gaul? And even then the beautiful dream doesn't die. Others keep searching for Quivira and reading the golden books. Indeed, it would be more than half a century after Coronado's return before Cervantes could begin to smile away that antique literature of chivalry and romance (and in doing so, write the first modern novel) and almost a century until Velázquez would invert the hierarchy of myth and reality in the Spanish mind by painting the *picaros* of the Madrid dives as Bacchus's boon companions and Venus showing the backside of a real woman to a real world.

7

Autumn, 1992. In a café somewhere off Bancroft Avenue, Walt Whitman, the Great Literatus, sits absent-mindedly dipping his beard in a cold latte while outside the citizens of Berkeley, California, jerk and jump forward in the worn-out sprockets of God's waning attention. A hundred years before, the Great Literatus had imagined Columbus, old, sick, and in disgrace, vouchsafed a final vision of his quest complete:

> Shadowy vast shapes smile through the air and sky,
> And on the distant waves sail countless ships,
> And anthems in new tongues I hear saluting me.

Vision, dream, reality? Who knows? It is a momentous event, and the Great Literatus ponders it, the girdling of the globe, East and West joined once-more, that journey back to the mystical source that could only be made along a western arc. Again and again in his mind (in reality he never got farther than Denver) Whitman had made the trek west, his teeth jostled in his head as he sat in the box of some creaking covered wagon or sped along the gleaming parallel rails. Time and again he had washed his feet in the Pacific and imagined the great Soul Journey over, the Passage to India complete, the great circle that began in Eden closed. Once, in 1955, Allen Ginsberg thought he caught sight of him in a Berkeley supermarket, a "childless, lonely old grubber, poking among the meats in the refrigerator and eyeing the grocery boys," as if sheer longing had drawn him to this coast.

Forget the massacred natives, the burned villages, and leveled civilizations. Forget the forests of hacked stumps, the ravaged mountains, and poisoned rivers. Forget the wake of bribed congressmen and swindled legislatures and used-up Chinese and Irish workers that the twin lines of gleaming steel trailed behind them. In Walt Whitman had surged the Divine Afflatus, he had dilated with his great poem and invented a language (he called it his barbaric yawp) capacious enough to include the very noise and clash of the young land, *the blab of the pave, tires of carts, sluff of bootsoles.* It was the language of Caliban trying to remember Prospero's incantations (or, more shrewdly, it was Prospero disguised as Caliban and singing through Walt Whitman's pores) and the poem had grown in the poet until his body itself had become the poem, love-root, silk-thread, crotch and vine, root of wash'd sweet-flag! timorous pond-snipe!

But having arrived on this mystical shore, the Literatus hesitated. His poem, like mist-hidden Cíbola, like that Quivira that wandered across the map from the pueblos of New Mexico to the Oregon coast, had become unmoored. And the Literatus lapsed for a moment into a kind of forgetfulness:

> Long having wander'd since, round the earth having wandered,
> Now I face home again, very pleas'd and joyous,
> (But where is what I started for so long ago?
> And why is it yet unfound?)

But be careful what you're dreamin' –
soon your dreams'll be dreamin' you.
Willie Nelson, "It's Not Supposed to Be That Way"

Dream Mining

We sit in the living room of his duplex apartment and he tells me of the
Dream Mine and the signs of its fulfillment. As he speaks, the white ankles
of his Temple Garments peek out from under his trouser cuffs. Perhaps he
continues to wear his Garments out of spite: he has been ostracized so-
cially, religiously, matrimonially – "cut off," as he puts it. Such is the awful
burden of dreaming.

"What we missed," he says, "is that the mine couldn't come in until it
was legal to own gold in this country." He says this with the hard voice and
declamatory eyebrows of prophetic certainty. All the times they misread
the signs of the Mine's coming, the premature fanfares of the past – these
only confirm the exactness of the prophecy. But now the day is surely at
hand. I think a little uneasily of the morning's headlines and the grim tid-
ings of the financial page. Such gloom is good news to the Dreamers, who
will have the satisfaction of being up when we are down, of being vindicated while the rest of us are being proved so very, very wrong. Who will
have the Mine when we have nothing. So I sit there and he tells me of the
mysterious "red money" that will replace a dollar devalued to twenty cents
of its current worth and that even now is printed and ready for distribution. How this red money itself will be worthless. He expounds for me the
ominous "Republican Elephant Dream" of the original seer, Bishop John

Koyle. He tells me of the devastations of armies and the collapse of governments and the 700-degree heat that will *separate the wheat from the tares.* It sets you to thinking, this sort of talk. I ask him if he's ever had any supernatural testimony of the Mine's reality himself. "I never had to," he says. "I never had any doubts that needed to be proved." He personally looks for the end of the world as we know it with the coming of spring.

Through the living-room window rises the white, snowy granite saddle of one of the last peaks of the Wasatch. On the wall to my right there is a painting of the same wintery mountain. I cannot see the Dream Mine mountain from the window, but I know it is out there, hidden by the shoulder of the saddle peak. And there is a painting of it, too, in the living room. A soft, twilit summer scene. It is Sunday in this slow Mormon town and only the two of us are not in church, myself – a gentile – and this aging excommunicate, who continues to weave his dense net of scripture and prophecy in the somnolent atmosphere. I look from the snow-covered peak in the window to the painting on the wall and wonder if we are seeing the same mountain out there. It may take more than the turn of another spring to know. But they are good at waiting, these Dreamers. They have been doing it, after all, since 1894. Screwed into the frame of the painting of the Dream Mine mountain is a plaque with the first line of Psalm 121: I will lift up mine eyes unto the hills, from whence cometh my help.

..

The Dream Mine exists in a tantalizing mental area between fiction and reality. It *is* there, a palpable, concrete presence: a cone-shaped granite mountain with a mine shaft sunk 1,400 feet into its heart and roads and grades and a modern three-tiered plant for extracting the ore and bins for its storage. But not an ounce of gold or anything else of much monetary value has come out of the mine in its hundred-year history. For the Dream Mine is really an idea. It is an idea that has affected the lives of perhaps 35,000 people. Believers are not ashamed to call themselves "Dreamers" or "Dream Miners." They speak of being "converted to the Mine." For them it is a morality, a theology, a testing. A spiritual burden that has been born by their fellowship for three generations. And yet the Dream Mine remains stubbornly worldly, a spiritual investment in which you can literally buy shares. Just when you think you can put your hand on the Dream Mine, it eludes you.

Perhaps the simplest place to begin, beyond folklore or the psychology of mass hallucination, is to see the Dream Mine as a survival of primitive

Mormonism. Above the smug Cartesian streets of Salt Lake City the golden Angel Moroni still balances with one foot just touching the spires of the Mormon Temple, the trumpet announcing the end of the World of the Flesh hovering before his lips. But Mormonism is a millenarian religion which has ceased, except in a pro forma sort of way, to be millenarian. The grounds below the Angel are still crowded with people, but these are more apt to be tourists than zealots. The strange nineteenth-century Vermont Gothic of the Temple, with its spires and granite gingerbread, and the Angel himself are dwarfed by the efficient, relentlessly corporate lines of the Church office building across the way, and in the new Visitor's Center the curious are treated not to the thunders and prophecy that once rang through Mormondom, but to polite little lectures in front of waxwork tableaux. The Church has become a success upon the face of the earth. It no longer preaches the troublesome doctrines of polygamy or the divinely inspired and directed communism of the United Order. It no longer prints its own money or talks secession from the Union. It no longer prophesies or talks in tongues. It has become a comfortable part of middle America. It is as if the Saints had quietly agreed to defer the hot breath and clamorous trumpets of the Latter Days. But something is missing here, something that isn't to be found in the bland, young faces and eager handshakes of the ranks of missionaries (who sometimes seem to be door-to-door salesmen for some alternate form of life insurance) or in the Church basketball program or on the teeming campus of Brigham Young University or in Family Home Evening. It is something that thrives ill in all this comfort and seeks out hard luck and loneliness and dry diggings. It has a hint of brimstone about it and pioneer toughness. You can call it Vision.

To understand the original call of a religion, look at its heresies. Take a look at the landscape that gives them its prophets. So I drive south of Salt Lake City, between the edge of the Jordan River Valley and the snowy spine of the Wasatch Mountains, then down the east shore of Provo Lake and into the Dream Mine land.

It is a country fit for dreaming. Towns here have names like Goshen, Salem, Lehi, names that come from the Bible, the Book of Mormon. The last peaks of the Wasatch rise abruptly from the high plateau, rough sheets of granite, glacier-scarred and sudden and intensely beautiful. Across the broad, flat plain to the west lie the softer, more feminine peaks of the Oquirrhs, whose subtle folds have a mystical way of catching the light and transforming it. The valley itself is open at both ends. To the south lies the bleak sagebrush prairie called the Levan Desert; to the north an endless, mirage-haunted expanse of salt flats and then the Great Salt Lake itself, level and dead and vast. It is the kind of country where a passing cloud can shadow the desert floor around you or ride a sudden puff of wind across a field of new hay and fill a whole afternoon with foreboding. In this stark light the simplest objects can take on a profound significance: the way a split-rail fence runs along an empty field or the shape of a horse or cow standing against the noon sun or a hay derrick idle against a spavined barn. A jackrabbit scared up in a sagebrush swale can change the entire texture of a day. Now the desert vastness is filled to some extent with the glut of end-of-the-century America, the little Mormon towns have cafés and dime stores and ranch-style houses alongside the old high-peaked adobe and native stone schools and meeting houses; but the emptiness is so great you can never fill it all, the light still plays its tricks with you, and under the thin scab of civilization it is still the same hard country it was in 1886 when a spiritually troubled young Mormon farmer named John Koyle had his first dream.

Norman C. Pierce, the late historian of these events, put it like this:

Then he dreamed a strange dream in which he saw that his cow, which had been lost for several days, had wandered down by his lower field, and that somehow she had been into some trouble so that her right horn was broken and bent over, with the point of it sticking into her eye. And there he was able to see her now in this vivid dream, in a place that he at once clearly recognized. Then a voice spoke out of the dream and said "If you find your cow in this place tomorrow, will you believe that the Restored Gospel is true?"

And unhesitatingly, John seemed to say "Yes sir." The next day Koyle found his cow where he had dreamed he would. Her right horn had been caught in a fence and had broken and the point was sticking into her eye. It was a strangely humble dream, judged by the standards of Koyle's later visions, yet it takes us back to a uniquely spiritualized world, a world where there was no border between the real and the supernatural, where these empty desert valleys were truly the land of Zion and God and his ministering angels had their hands in even the most mundane aspects of every-day life. A world where the Three Nephites, deathless survivors of the Hebrew tribes that Joseph Smith had seen peopling primitive America, still went abroad doing their secret charities and you could meet them on a country road or find a gold piece under a plate where you'd fed a stranger and know they'd been by; a world where a Mormon elder could have a waking vision settling some point of doctrine or community quarrel or telling him where to plant his peas. And a man like John Koyle would stand in the door of his adobe hut or lean over the beam of his plow and look into that immense desert light and think and consult the signs. So he thought about his cow.

He must have done a lot of thinking. Eight years after his initial vision, one night in late August, he had another dream, and this one was wonderful to behold. He dreamed that an angel in white came to him and led him to a mountain east of his home in Leland. After climbing halfway up its side, the two of them entered the mountain itself. In an eerie sort of corporal disintegration they passed through more than 1,000 feet of solid rock and into the mountain's heart. And, as they went, the angel in white pointed out to John Koyle the features of the different rock formations and strata, features which years later he was to claim he could recall with perfect fidelity. At the core of the mountain the rock turned to a rich white quartz veined thick with gold – veins so pure that, as Koyle later put it, they were "like fish with their heads off and their entrails out, ready for the frying pan." Then they plunged directly earthward. About 175 feet down they came to a cluster of nine large caverns and there they found a strange clutter of ancient artifacts – hieroglyphs, vases, tools – and yet more gold, gold minted into coins and stamped into thick plates containing the sacred records of a vanished people. For this was a mine belonging to the race of Nephites and the angel in white was that same Angel Moroni who a little over sixty years earlier had visited Joseph Smith and had given him the golden records of the lost Hebraic people who, in Mormon doctrine, had inhabited America millennia ago. In a sadly beautiful metamorphosis, the angel in white was to transform himself into that haunting cream-colored vein of rock which, twisting and turning always deeper, the Dream Miners were to follow into the heart of the mountain for the next forty years.

Sometime after this spectacular dream, and after still more spiritual prompting, Koyle went up on the Dream Mountain with a certain Joseph Brockbank and found the place where he had entered the mountain with the angel. A halo of light glowed over it, although it was high noon. But still Koyle hesitated, until one day – in the humble workings of such signs – he awoke to find all his chickens dead. Let Norman Pierce finish the story: "Then, as some of his children became quite ill, his wife exclaimed, 'For goodness sake, John, get up on the hill and go mining, before the children die too. This is enough of a warning for me.'" The Koyle Mining Company was incorporated on 4 March 1909, under the laws of the State of Utah. The original issue of stock was 114,000 shares, of which 42,000 shares, at a par value of $1.00 were offered to the public for $1.50 each. The Dream Mine had begun its curious career between revelation and speculation. Koyle, who could talk like a live-wire salesman, as well as a seer, when he had to, put the goals of the company into terms of "The Three M's: Mining, Minting and Manufacturing." It was, as will be seen, a rather optimistic motto. But already the Dream Miners had begun to drill and blast their way into the mountain.

It is necessary to see the Dream Mine as a sort of mental fossil of a time and place. The era of John Koyle's trials and visions was one of Utah mineral strikes scarcely less fabulous than the one of which he dreamed, made, often, by men hardly more likely. In the Tintic district, where Koyle sold his butter and eggs, a Mormon magnate named Jesse Knight had gambled and won on a mine so unpromising it was called the Humbug. The Humbug had been located in a dream two years after Koyle claimed his own mine vision. The Book of Mormon itself was sprinkled with references to the treasures hidden by the lost peoples of this continent, and a Dreamer might well quote you Helaman 13:19–20, say, or Mormon 1:18–19 to assuage any lingering doubts you might have about the Mine. After all, Joseph Smith had, in his less respectable days, been a digger of buried treasure, a peepstone augur of the secrets hid beneath the earth. Nor was the Dream Mine mixture of prophecy and profit so odd to Mormon ears of this later time. Hadn't God himself once charged the Prophet, Seer, and Revelator Joseph to invest in a boarding house? Even so, the Dream Mine movement did not sit well with official Mormonism. For visionary religions have the strange tendency to turn the kind of people who were the seers and prophets of the first generation into the cranks and embarrassments of the third and fourth. In 1896, two years after Koyle's visit from the angel, Utah finally became a state. The price the Mormon establishment had paid in its long quest for legitimacy was the final abandonment of most of those doctrines that had made it an unassimilable morsel in the gullet of America. The handful of dusty little utopias of the United Order were allowed to lapse back into welfare capitalism like the rest of Mormon Utah, polygamy itself became heresy, and unregenerate polygamous elders posed for photographs in the stripes of the state penitentiary.

On 10 January 1914, at 5 A.M. Mountain Time, John Koyle, ousted from his Bishopric, at odds with his Church, was once more paid a preternatural visit. And this time his visitors left him with a message. What these two white bearded men in gray told John Koyle (for the record, they turned out to be two of the ageless Three Nephites — it was the shorter Nephite who did most of the talking) can only be known in part, for Koyle was sworn to reveal only a half hour of the two-hour conversation to the general public and only one and one half hours to the Church authorities themselves. He never was given a chance to make this latter revelation, but the half-hour conversation turned the Dream Mine from a speculation to a moral and theological enterprise. For the Mine was henceforth to be a Relief Mine, a haven of refuge in a disaster that was soon to be visited on an erring race. In that season of trial would come four years of drought and famine when governments would crumble and economies nose-dive and "Church, State and Nation in rapid sequence will be brought up a standin' to judgement like a wild colt to a snubbin' post," as John Koyle later liked to say. The Mine would become the first in a chain of Cities of Refuge. Here the vindi- cated stockholders would gather, a sort of fiduciary elect, recuperating from the disaster and distributing alms to the faithless from their now bur- geoning mint and storehouses. But the Mine would be more than that. It would be a step to something beyond mere material survival. For it was destined to reinstate plural marriage in the land of Zion and in its mille- narian atmosphere the United Order would be realized on earth. "Here in these cities of Zion there would be no rich and no poor. They would share in the resources of the community according to their needs and render ser- vices according to their abilities. And by the end of the four years of drought and famine, we will progress to a state where we know how to live without money under the law of total consecration." Once more, these words are those of Mine historian Norman Pierce. A short time after the visit of the Nephites, the Dream Mine was shut down on pain of excom- munication by a nervous Church establishment. It was to remain shut for six years.

In 1920 the Mine was allowed to reopen because of a legal technicality: a $2,000 debt owed by the Dream Miners to the Spanish Fork Church Co- Operative. Once reopened, the Mine was to remain open for almost thirty years. The bad days of the Depression were in fact good days for the Mine. Koyle's prophecies of final doom seemed ever closer to fulfillment: they were coming true now. The Mine itself, beyond even the hopes of its future bonanza, was a sort of solution. The expanding band of believers bought stock when they could afford it or worked for it at the rate of three shares per day on the suddenly feverishly active slopes of the Mountain. For the Mine, barren as it appeared, was to serve as a kind of moral test for the Dreamers in Koyle's new vision: only when the Mine *itself* was ready, would it deliver its treasure. Until then the Dreamers dug and prayed and dug and prayed, going ever deeper into the cold, empty heart of granite.

At first the Church chose to fight this heresy in its midst with, for it, an odd tool: science. Dr. James E. Talmage, eminent geologist and Church leader, visited the Mine in order to denounce it. He was promptly asked if he was denouncing it in his role as Apostle or geologist. After some hesitation he said as Apostle. Dr. Frederick J. Pack of the University of Utah was less hesitant. He ended a review of Dream Mine samples in the Salt Lake City *Deseret News* of 20 January 1933 by saying that he didn't find a single productive vein within the entire property. To his friends Pack put it more bluntly: "You can get more values out of the dirt sweepings on the main streets of Salt Lake City than you can out of ore from the Dream Mine." Two state prosecutions for fraud and a Securities and Exchange Commission investigation failed to halt the Mine. The SEC was forced to conclude that there was no evidence of fraud, since the improvements at the mine were more valuable than the money taken in by the company, and the stockholders were satisfied.

The stockholders were satisfied. Here it is in its nakedness, the truth about Dream Mining, the heart of the mystery. For such is the horrible economy of dreams that the dream is self-cannibalizing, it feeds on the stuff of its own illusions. Only the Dream Mine itself can unlock its ore; each painful inch of gain made into the indifferent heart of the mountain, each round of holes laboriously drilled and blasted *might* be the round that will deliver the Mine (but never does), each dry shaft and broken drill and caved-in stope only confirms the purity of the dream, and hope is measured in negative increments. The Dream Mine is the dark side of America.

And yet it is America's best promise too, for now it is the Great Depression, remember. Thus in 1930 the Dreamers somehow manage to start terracing the grain bins and storehouses of the coming City of Refuge. In 1932, miraculously, they raise enough cash to begin work on the concentrating plant. And in 1937 the mine produces its first – and almost its last – income: a check for $103.03 from a Chicago company for a shipment of selenium and iron hydroxide. Not even the deaths of three miners in the Mine's thirty-some years have dampened enthusiasm. Mass meetings fill the Spanish Fork High School Auditorium and generate enough money to install pumps and agitators and pulverizers and graduated crushers at the mill house. They have not yet mined a pinch of gold ore. But the Mine doesn't come in after all, and hope turns in upon itself like a rotten toenail. By the late 1940s Dream Mining had become a kind of closet heresy: you get the impression that some of the best Mormon families still kept their shares tucked away, although they didn't like to talk about it.

I have seen two photographs of Bishop Koyle. In the first he has the amiable, jowly look of a successful automobile salesman. His mustache is white and trim, his eyes have a gleam in them that is to the viewer more like that of a glad-handing Rotarian than a prophet. Perhaps this was taken in the good days of the "platinum boom," when rumors of a strike sent Dream Mine stock up to ten dollars a share. Perhaps it is the gleam of 1939, the Mine's "Year of Prosperity." In the other photograph John Koyle has changed. It is taken, as I judge, just before his death. The cheeks are sunken, the face has turned thin, the mustache droops. He is in his work clothes, perhaps just come out of the mountain. You can see the dirt of the mine on his face. His eyes are remarkable. This was his time of trial. On 8 January 1947, Koyle was called before the High Council of Twelve in Spanish Fork and the formal process of his excommunication was begun. Raymond Taylor, one of the council, has left an unpublished account of the trial. Each of the twelve drew a number from a hat, the odd to defend Koyle, the even to present the case against him. Two of the men who had drawn odd numbers exchanged them for even; they had sold Koyle mining equipment. By the time the trial was over Koyle had signed a statement denying the primacy of his own revelation and yielding to the Church authority in all particulars. Henceforth the Koyle Mining Company was to be considered a business speculation only, divorced from all mystery. Koyle was old and sick and he wanted to die in the Church. It is said that when he heard the council's decision he wept.

But the dream hardens around you. It is intolerant of your petty needs, your watching, your humanity. It is a Mountain. And so, in April of 1948, Koyle was again hailed into the High Council. Now the charge was insubordination. The Church hierarchy had gone back on its promise to Koyle not to make his abjuration public and had published it prominently in the *Deseret News*. To Koyle this nullified his own promise to keep his mining enterprise secular. Raymond Taylor participated in this second council session as well. There Koyle freely admitted to having a meeting at the Mine of "about a hundred, where they did bear testimonies, sing songs of Zion and certain speakers quoted from the scriptures and bore their testimonies in the name of Jesus Christ, etc. etc." Once more the twelve drew lots. "It was a very interesting and unsavory experience," Taylor writes. "It really stirred me. I didn't sleep that night at all after the affair." This time there was no abjuration and no weeping. After the decision of excommunication was announced, Koyle called down the judgment of God upon the Council of Twelve in an eloquent manner. "I loved that part of the meeting and admired his spunk," Taylor continues. "The old boy had plenty of spunk and pluck left in him." As the old man was going out the door Taylor took him by the arm and said "Brother Koyle! Now you can have that hearing before the First Presidency. It is your legal right now." I do not believe the hearing ever took place. A year later, on 17 May 1948, Koyle died excommunicate. He was buried in his Temple Garments, as he wished.

..

And so on a January day twenty-seven years after John Koyle's death, eighty-one years after his first Visitation (for Dream Miners like to keep such temporal references in order,) I found myself parked at the edge of a snowy field near a little swale and looking up at the Dream Mine Mountain itself.

Like all dreams it hadn't been easy to find, and now that I had, it was a little disappointing. It was a little too definite, a little too geographically placed and etched on that brittle winter day. A conical heap of granite and glacial talus at the end of the Wasatch. John Koyle's Dream Mountain. As I looked, I could just make out the half-buried line of the dugway zigzagging through the snow, what I thought might be the corrugated tin roof of the mill. I looked back, across the valley behind me and into the Jordan Narrows. And I thought how just before he died, when everything had fallen apart, John Koyle was supposed to have looked out there and had one final vision. What he saw was "a small rift in the dark clouds revealing a little spot of blue about the size of a man's hand." Then, as he watched, this spot of blue expanded, the skies opened and "the mine and its surroundings were restored to the brilliant sunshine of a fine, glorious day, with all oppressiveness having vanished away." So I looked out, and all I could see was the long, dirty plume of smoke hanging over the Magna copper mill at the edge of the lake, the low band of smog that hugged the roots of the Oquirrhs. I turned back in the direction of the mine. Two faint tracks led down the swale and up the mountain. They were covered with ice and narrow and although I had a four-wheel-drive car, I was alone. Besides, I had seen enough boarded-up mine entrances in my life, and rusted ore cars and flooded shafts.

How many true believers in the Mine remain is difficult to tell. The Dreamers are themselves evasive about this. When they gather for their annual stockholders meeting on the second Monday in May they are, as has been described to me, mostly old people, not enough to make up a quorum, so the present Board of Directors continues in office without election. The Mine itself is once more shut down and awaits divine intervention to reopen. The Dreamers continue to hold on to their shares and study the world for the omens by which Bishop Koyle said they would know the end was at hand: the hot, dry summer, the four years of drought and famine, the financial crash. And they look out across this haunting desert valley for the rift of blue in the dark clouds about the size of a man's hand. Every spring they plant their truck garden at the base of the mountain, weed it, and water it through the summer in order to pay the assessment on the mine and keep up the claim. Some of them are at cross-lots with each other, but few openly challenge the Church anymore. As one Dreamer said to me, "When you discover a truth in the scripture, store it up in your mind like a hidden treasure." They look to the signs, keep their own counsel, and wait for a time when the Mine will come in, when the mountain "will look like an anthill, people begging for stock." Bishop Koyle too will return in the flesh, they say, to enjoy his vindication in a cleansed and redeemed land where there will be no rich and no poor and the righteous will enjoy plural marriage as did the Saints of old, a kingdom truly on earth as it is in Heaven. "One of the most difficult elements to deal with was the wishful thinking each of us did when contemplating the destiny of this mine and how it would influence our lives, and in turn the lives of others," wrote Norman Pierce. "Without the eternal hope and expectancy of success in the next few rounds of holes very few people would have parted so readily with the necessary money to satisfy the needs of the pursuance of this great work." For those who have kept the faith perhaps it is this "eternal hope" that is the real treasure of the mine. Who's to say?

Like so many other lost mines and buried treasures of the West, the Dream Mine sits on the uneasy borders of folklore and geology. And may sit there still. Intractable mirage that it is, now and then the Mine resurfaces in the press. In 1985, an article in *Utah Holiday* traced the current status of the mine through the netherworld of failed ponzi schemes and scary apostate Mormon fundamentalists. The old believers continue to die off, one by one. The Mine will be there as long as there are dreams and money. For, after all, isn't that what it is about?

..

So I never did get up to the Dream Mine, after all. Coming back to Salt Lake, I decided to swing through the little town of Salem, at the foot of the mountain. Ward meeting was just getting out. The Ward House was new, a sterile, California-like structure of cream-colored brick on the model of all the new wards. It could have been a suburban insurance agency or a freeway restaurant. Kids filled the muddy street, the preteen girls in short skirts and tights, the boys with the modishly long hair they were wearing that year. That was something you wouldn't have seen a few years earlier down here. The town was ugly: a few squat brick houses of the 1920s and the newer cheap ranch models of the 1950s cramped next to each other on little lots. Here and there, crowded among them, was a severe old high-peaked farmhouse of plastered adobe from the 1870s. In a backyard or two you found other small evidences of the Mormon frontier, the low mound of a root cellar or a log-and-chink smokehouse. At the edge of the freeway there was a sign for a defunct housing tract. It was called "Dream View Acres." I pulled on to the interstate and cast a quick look at the snowy ridge of mountains to the east, a kind of perfunctory farewell. I really preferred the painting over Mr. Pierce's fireplace, the mountain shown on one of those soft, late summer evenings that seemed to suspend themselves forever in the desert air, with the last of the light turning the foothills pale violet and touching for a moment with a dying finger of sun the dim zigzag of the dugway, the roof of the mill. It is, perhaps, that last long evening of summer before the millennial dawn. Things were looking up for the Dreamers. That coming Wednesday Mr. Norman Pierce was to speak to the Spanish Fork Lions Club. The subsidiary silver mine in Nevada had already struck ore, so the Dreamers said, and they were just waiting for the snow to clear to bring it out. The spring planting for the truck garden might presage a harvest of hope, the May stockholders' meeting might be stormed by investors eager to buy in. As I drove north I tried to recall the conclusion of the poem "Victory" by the Dreamer Carter Grant. Later on I checked my notebook and found the lines I was thinking about.

It was a vision, a vision of the End of Time, the terrified unbelievers

70

swarming up to the "mountain fortress" that was the Mine, feverish, begging for stock. And then the awful words:

It's too late friends, there's none for you!

When at last the values burst forth there would be no stock in my hand. The books were sealed, fastened; Yes, if it did come, that final triumph, that sudden glory up at the Mine, I would not be there. I would be one of those desperate procrastinators clambering up the steep sides of the mountain, the grit of our disbelief thrown back in our teeth. I knew for sure I was one of the tares.

Cowboys, Wobblies, and the Myth of the West

I

This is how we prefer to see him, standing alone in the long sundown of our collective imagination, the false-front stores and board sidewalks retreating to the margins of our consciousness, a man now nothing more than a heroic silhouette rising from the lengthening shadows of Main Street as if snipped out of the history that falls away and out of the picture. Homeless, ancestorless, his name itself is a kind of genre, his presence is as ancient and unanswerable as the granite peaks that catch the last of the dying light beyond him.

In a moment it is all over. Trampas lies dead at the other end of Main Street and the Virginian (for it is he), rides off to the tall timber: a Western myth has crystallized into its final form.

Like any myth, the Western myth is an artifact, a tool made by human beings to do a certain work. Yet every artifact – potsherd, weapon, popular novel – raises an appropriate question: whom does it serve, and who pays the price? This particular myth of the West, as a tool for the distortion of historical reality, was paid for by the laboring men and women whose lives and struggles it attempted to devalue or deny. But in doing so, it called up a countermyth, a myth of the western worker that matched and opposed it in its view of human possibility, that parodied it when it had to, and erected its own version of an imagined future. This countermyth is embed-

73

ded in the ideology, the propaganda – in the very style – of that most radical of labor and political movements, the i.w.w., the Industrial Workers of the World. We will come to the Wobblies by and by; but first we must look at how Owen Wister and his fellow patrician mythmakers forced their distortions upon the lives of those western workers central to their project, the cowboys. For in assimilating these saddle-hardened young men into their own scheme of things, they had their work cut out for them.

..

In 1881 President Chester A. Arthur, in his First Annual Message to Congress, was asking for authority to deal with "a band of armed desperadoes known as Cowboys" who were disturbing the tranquillity of Arizona Territory. Just seven years later, Theodore Roosevelt, who would ride to the presidency in part by projecting his mystique as a man of the West, was picturing the cowboys thusly:

Singly, or in twos or threes, they gallop their wiry little horses down the street, their lithe, supple figures erect or swaying slightly as they sit loosely in the saddle; while their stirrups are so long that their knees are hardly bent, the bridles not taut enough to keep the chains from clanking. They are smaller and less muscular than the wielders of ax and pick; but they are as heady and self-reliant as any man who ever breathed – with bronzed, set faces, and keen eyes that look all the world straight in the face without flinching as they flash out from under the broad-brimmed hats. Peril and hardship, and years of long toil broken by weeks of brutal dissipation, draw haggard lines across their eager faces, but never dim their reckless eyes nor break their bearing of self-confidence.

These aestheticized cowboys, these horseback dandies, are servants of an ideology that had been imported to the West whole, an ideology which would, in the Western, seek more and more to be disguised in myth. Molding itself to its function of disguise, it was a myth made up as much of absences as presences. What was absent from the cowboy myth was the racial competition between men who were not only "Saxon boys of picked courage" as Roosevelt's friend and the author of The Virginian, Owen Wister, had it, but African Americans, Hispanics, Native Americans, Mixed-bloods. What was absent, or at best, barely sketched in, were the mines, railroads, and timber mills where immigrant workers were making the West into an economic extension of eastern U.S. and European capital. Above all, what was absent was the work. To be sure, there were descriptions of roundups and branding and stampedes, there were elegant draw-

74

ings by Frederic Remington of bronc busters and line riders, but work as a condition, as economic necessity, as a psychology, was scarcely present. Roosevelt, Wister, Remington – the Easterners who wrote the books and drew the drawings kept the fancy shirts and the whoop and bravado, but preferred to forget that the cowboys were workers – and marginal, dependent workers at that. To see the underside of the cowboy myth one must look elsewhere.

In a sense, you find the West you are looking for. Wister, Remington, Roosevelt found theirs among the primitives of Wyoming and the Dakotas. Karl Marx's daughter found hers in a Cincinnati Dime Museum. It was there, in 1886, that Eleanor Marx Aveling and her husband Edward came across a group of disgruntled young cowboys.

The cowboys "were sitting in twos and threes on various little raised platforms, clad in their picturesque garb, and looking terribly bored." It is a poignant image. Having lost their chance to be men (were they survivors of the cowboy strike of 1885 on Wyoming's Sweetwater?), the cowboys are now reduced to an exhibit, a sideshow curiosity.

After a stereotyped spiel by a barker, one of the cowboys, John Sullivan, "*alias* Broncho John," made a speech, the gist of which, much to the surprise of Eleanor Marx Aveling, was a denunciation of capitalists in general and ranch owners in particular. At a private talk the next day, the Avelings learned even more. They learned of the dangerous work; the sleepless, hungry nights chasing stampeded herds; the bad pay; the cost of the cowboy's gear. Of ranchers' blacklists, and the dreadful economy of the trail. "The rule is," Broncho John said, "the cowboy must fatten the cattle on the trail, *no matter how thin he may grow himself.*" Strip a cowboy of his horse – he rarely owned it anyway – and what was he but one more seasonal worker, attached to the industrial world by railroads that led to Chicago stockyards and ranches owned as often as not by eastern bankers or Scottish investors.

I fogged them caddle, an' I fogged 'em hard,

one song went,

An' I eat sowbelly 'til I shit pure lard,
Singin' "Tie, yie, yippy, yappy, yay!"

Badly fed and badly paid, the cowboy was little higher in status than a tramp, wandering from ranch to ranch in search of a job or driving another man's beef to another man's railroad for salt pork, beans, and forty dollars a month. When one young Texas cowboy went to settle up with the outfit for which he'd been working almost two years, the ranch storekeeper laid out 300 dollars on the counter, then promptly deducted everything but seventy-five cents for charges against his wage. The cowboy blew the seventy-five cents on peach liquor and stick candy and rode away.

..

For Roland Barthes, myths – specifically, the myths of modern capitalism – were mechanisms to obscure a process by which what is historical is made "natural." They are disguised ideology. In Owen Wister's *The Virginian,* the source from which all subsequent streams of the Western flow, the process is not complete: ideology and mythology exist side by side and it is a tribute to the power of myth that in our memories its solvent washes away the ideology and leaves only a few stark images: the lone cowboy, the gunfight, the famous retort, "when you call me that, *smile.*" Yet to read *The Virginian* again is to see its mythmaking contingent on, and at the service of, its ideology. But just what is it that this ideology strives to justify or push forward?

One way of reading *The Virginian* is as a defense of the brutal events of the Johnson County War of 1892, in which the major cattle ranchers of Wyoming banded together to crush the small settlers who were fencing the range. Under the guise of a civilizing war, the ranchers brought a small army of hired Texas gunmen north to wipe out this gang of "rustlers," whom they claimed the elected county officials and courts were protecting. Openly expressed, the ideology of *The Virginian* is an apology for lynch law in a frontier situation where vigilantism is the only law that "works." Yet by the time *The Virginian* saw print in 1902, the Johnson County War that had caused Wister's rancher friends from the tennis courts of the Cheyenne Club such embarrassment was ten years past. For Wister the "frontier" West was already a memory in *The Virginian.* The "historical" events of the book had already taken on a certain metaphoric quality. The book is by its own admission a work of nostalgia, a kind of evocation of a West that has forever fled. But nostalgia, which sets its face backwards, is always a disguise for the present, for present longings and present concerns.

Projected on the screen of a West that had already outlived its frontier past, the cowboy myth that the men of the East were perfecting was a kind of coded language for their real project. Its racism was another justification for the imperial pretensions that men like Theodore Roosevelt would do so much to promote; its cult of the cowboy individualist a sort of forlorn wish for an "innocent" capitalism far from the tooth-and-claw economics of Wall Street and the Trusts so busy creating fortunes for the few and misery for the many. The Virginian himself, at first glance that splendid, free-spirited pagan, is, on closer examination, a gunman, a racist, and the promoter of a convenient kind of Social Darwinism that pitted the "expert" against lesser men and justified success by any means. When it comes to choose between lynch law and a democracy overrun by poor settlers and Populist cowboys, the Virginian chooses the rope. And, in the end, Wister's free-spirited knight of the prairie, the "natural man" of the West, turns out to be, under his well-worn stetson, a Christian, a frugal saver, and an incipient capitalist who has had the foresight to locate his homestead on coal lands. What's more, we discover that all along he has been investing in "proper" clothes with which to pay genteel visits. He even – so much for the myth – ends up married. In short, Wister calms his eastern audience by assuring them that in spite of the six guns and chaps the Virginian is no threat to either their morals or their ideology, but rather is their defender. In fact, the Virginian is only another version of themselves. For this "natural" man is poised against an alien invasion:

"There go some more I-talians."

"They're Chinese," said Trampas.

"That's so," acknowledged the Virginian with a laugh. . . . Without cheap foreigners they couldn't afford all this hyeh new gradin'."

In Wister's and in Roosevelt's writings the industrial workers who populate the West are scarcely seen. They are voiceless presences, ghosts, and when we do catch a glimpse of them it is usually to contrast them disparagingly with the romantic and independent cowboys. Wister's fictional violence against the rustlers can be read as a code for that ominous violence his audience held in readiness against a whole other group – a group they found more disturbing than a handful of poor settlers and cowboys with running irons in far-off Wyoming. The workers – immigrant and native-born – so much an absence in the cowboy novel, so much a presence in the real West and in the minds of the Western's audience, are perceived by the very hole they leave in the Western's text, by the silence that wells up around them, not as the nonentities the myth held them to be, but in fact as a threat. Their absence in the fiction is an indication of the real concern of its middle-class audience, that visceral fear of being swamped by the tide of foreigners and foreign ideology being washed up on American shores.

In 1894 a part of this code was momentarily breached to reveal the real concern underneath. Frederic Remington, tireless weaver of the Western myth, friend and illustrator of both Wister and Roosevelt, was in Chicago. It was the time of the great Pullman Strike and the Panhandle Railyards were under virtual siege. Remington passed among the burning railroad cars and the strikers' barricades and expatiated on what he called the Chicago mob. For him the strikers were a "malodorous crowd of anarchistic foreign trash," and when what he called a "real workman" came out on the window landing of a factory and shook his fist at the mob, this scab's sentiments were quoted with Remington's full approval: "Kill 'em – kill every one of 'em, you soldiers; they are cowards; they 'ain't got no wives and children; they are cowardly whelps, and they do me harm who have a wife and children, and wants to make an honest living. Damn 'em, I wish I was a soldier."

Indeed, like the scab on the factory landing, Remington's sympathies are with the soldiers of the Seventh Cavalry, some of whom he had seen at Pine Ridge just after Wounded Knee. The soldiers would softly urge the "American" strikers to go home and not get shot; as for the others, "the Hungarian or Polack or whatever the stuff was" – "Say, do you know them things ain't human? – before God I don't think they are men." It is only the troops' presence which keeps "the social scum from rising to the top."

The iron logic that had justified the private army of Texas "regulators" in Johnson County in 1892 had in that same year justified the army of Pinkerton detectives at bloody Homestead, and would justify our imperialist policies both in the Philippines and in those interior colonies we continued to maintain, the dreary coal camps and mining towns of the West, and the foreigner-filled cities and factories of the East, where private detectives, state and federal troops, and citizen-vigilantes kept down insurrection. It was a logic embedded in the Western myth.

2

In the spring of 1913, twenty young men gathered in San Francisco to make their way by freight car to Denver, Colorado, 1,666 miles away. Although they would have to ride and camp across two major chains of mountains and a vast, bitter desert, they were traveling light: no blankets or bedrolls, but just such warm clothing as they could wear on their backs. They were the kind of young men who had traveled the rails by what they called the "side-door coach" often enough before, working stiffs moving from job to job in harvest fields or construction camps or in the forests of pine and spruce and Douglas fir. A number of them may have had skills, may have mined or carpentered or had any of a dozen different trades, but they would take what work they could find, and travel to it. Tramps or hobos the settled people of the towns might call them; they called themselves Wobblies. They were not traveling to a job now, not making that long trip for grub and a flop in some bug-ridden bunkhouse. They were traveling for an idea. With them they carried two signs. "On to Denver. Free Speech Denied the Right to Organize One Big Union" and "We are in your town and must eat."

This was not the first such Wobbly train. In Missoula, Montana, in Spokane, in Fresno, in San Diego, the i.w.w. had been fighting bloody battles with citizens committees and police for the right to stand up its soap-boxers with their revolutionary message on the streets where out-of-work men gathered among the saloons and flophouses and store-front labor agencies. Many of the San Francisco men were veterans of i.w.w. Free Speech clashes in those towns; on the way to Denver they would pick up twenty more men, all eager for the fight, including the seasoned organizer Frank Little, who would be lynched by vigilantes in Butte, Montana, four years later.

In Oroville, California, the Wobblies were locked up in jail briefly, but "the stay was timely as it afforded us some much needed rest." On the next stop they were not so lucky, and had to camp in the hobo jungles. Everywhere they went they sang Wobbly songs, sold leaflets, propagandized. In Elko, Nevada, they staged a sham free speech fight. "Our two cops, decorated with gigantic stars, had their troubles clubbing and man-handling the persistent soap boxers while the starvation army preyed [sic] peacefully a few feet away. It was a lesson in strife to those of us who have never felt the gentle touch of a grafter's club." Fifty-five miles from Salt Lake they were ditched in the desert with no blankets and very little to eat or drink. They sang "Mr. Block," "The White Slave," "The Red Flag," and other songs to keep warm. When they got to Salt Lake City the chief of police bawled out the cops who had brought them in, and the travelers "feasted" and bedded down in the i.w.w. hall. The next day they were herded onto a special express car to whisk them out of town. They were the third bunch of Wobblies who'd passed through. Nor was Provo, to the south, eager to treat with this little army. Then, at Green River, Utah, 200 miles from Salt Lake, came what Ed Nolan, the author of this account, called the real test of strength.

A Thing, resembling a gorilla, but far below that animal in intelligence, ordered sixty-five human workers, at the point of two massive forty some odd [revolvers], from the car. Its demands not being gratified, it became panic stricken, fear replacing bravado – cowardice crowning all – although backed by four nondescript business men, less brainy by far than the Thing. It wanted to stop us at Helper, Utah, but Helper wouldn't help.

How did we do it? Solidarity, gentle reader, Solidarity.

This moment, which was repeated on more than one Wobbly train, was a replay of the classic showdown on Main Street of *The Virginian*. But here the showdown is discredited, unmasked for what it is, and the myth is rewritten with another ending, to serve a different ideology.

To understand just what is going on, let us go back a few years.

1907. The men stand against the buildings, slouch hats and battered caps pulled down to keep the drizzle off their faces, a couple of blankets over their shoulders. On the corner the Salvation Army is drumming up trade, and there is a crowd around the blackboards of one of the employment shark's offices reading the notices of workers wanted. It is the "Slave Market." Spokane's Front Avenue, Market Street in Denver, Salt Lake's Second South, Chicago's West Madison. The men who stand in the rain are part of what Marx called the Industrial Reserve Army. They know who they are on more familiar terms: too many men for too few jobs for not enough pay. They are the same men from whom scabs and strikebreakers are recruited, bindle stiffs, harvest hands, out-of-work cowboys and miners, timber beasts. All alike in their gray sameness on the city streets or tramping the railroad right-of-ways and the roads, huddled around fires where the trains made up or took on water, almost invisible to ordinary people with comfortable lives. They know by heart the police interrogations:

Where you going'?
When was you born?
When, why and how?
What jail was you in last?

Come clean or I'll beat up on you till you tell.
I think I'll turn the hose on you.
Ain't you got any money?

They are there to do the necessary casual labor without which the farms
and industries cannot continue: harvesting, tree felling, seasonal construction work, anything that hands and backs can do. But the country treats
them with contempt – when it is not ignoring them. They are cheated by
employment sharks, sent out to jobs that don't exist or that dry up in a day
to be taken over by some other man; they are rousted out of their jungles
by Citizens' Committees and local cops, pushed off boxcars, shaken down
by brakemen and police, thrown into small-town jails when they can't buy
their way out of a vagrancy charge.

By 1920 one social critic claimed that practically half the men in Nevada, or
nearly 20,000 out of a total population of nearly 80,000, were living "under
bad social conditions outside the home environment, as cowboys, sheepherders, hay-hands, miners and railwaymen, sleeping in company bunk-
houses or on the range and dependent for their few pleasures and social con-
tacts on the frontier towns the traveler sees from the train window. These
afford a movie, perhaps, certainly a gambling house with bootleg whiskey,
and a 'restricted district' behind a stockade, in which the women are 'medi-
cally inspected' (for a price) while the men are not."

So numerous were these poor, wandering men in the West that the Mill-
er-Lux ranches, a cattle empire that stretched from Oregon and California
to the Great Basin, had a list of rules to guide their foremen.

Never refuse a tramp a meal, but never give him more than one.

Never refuse a tramp a night's lodging. Warn him not to use any matches
and let him sleep in the barn, but only for one night.

Never make a tramp work for his meal. He is too weak before and too
lazy afterwards.

Never let tramps eat with the men. Make them wait and eat off dirty plates.

The object of the rules was not charity. The rancher Miller claimed that
his policy saved him millions in fire insurance premiums. The handouts
were meant to pacify the wandering men; the dirty plates they ate from
told them who they were.

In the winter of 1891, a young Princeton graduate, a minister's son named Walter Wyckoff, was in Chicago trying to hook a job. Wyckoff had donned the clothes and adopted the life of the casual laborer for what he called a two-year "experiment in reality." His books are valuable for several reasons, but above all for the insight they give into the psychology of want. Hunger, the anxiety of joblessness, the fruitless search for work, had an effect on more than just the worker's belly and his outlook; they ate into his very sense of self. "Baffled and weakened, you are thrust back upon yourself and held down remorselessly to the cold, naked fact that you, who in all the universe are of supremest importance to yourself, are yet of no importance to the universe. You are a superfluous human being."

You are a superfluous human being: for the tramp, the migrant, this is the lesson that, more than any other, America's industrial system sought to teach. A stray job meant food, maybe a drink, and a momentary reintegration into the world of humanity, a momentary freedom from "the torment of that haunting isolation which keeps one unspeakably lonely even in the thronging crowd." But always there was the specter of failure, of hunger, and the hallucinatory repetition of asking for a job and being turned away, the eerie sense of having uttered the same words before. And always "the sense of being a thing apart in the presence of your working kind, a thing unvitalized by real contact with the streams of life, is the seat of your worst suffering, and the pain is augmented by what seems an actual antagonism to you as to something beyond the range of human sympathy."

It is this isolation, this loneliness that is the other side of the individualist coin that Wister and Roosevelt were trying to pass off in their myth of the West. Indeed, the alienation is a consequence of it. It is this myth that the Wobblies would try to undermine and reverse by a mythology of their own. Beyond the economic frontier that the i.w.w. was challenging, their project was a human one; their battle was a battle for consciousness. When those Denver-bound Wobblies faced down the pistol-slinging sheriff from Green River on that freight, what they were doing was more than just claiming a victory for people who had suffered from such gunmen and grafters in the past; they were claiming a right to make their own myths of themselves. In doing so they ironically reversed that man-to-man showdown on Main Street that stood for so much in Wister and his followers. The myth of the expert, that lone Westerner with the gun, was made ludicrous by its collision with the reality of the militant group. The Wobblies held that boxcar not in the name of the individual, and the whole ideology that individualism stood for, but in the name of another ideology, just as gripping, just as poetic, if the word can be allowed, and for the moment, more potent. Solidarity was their word for it.

3

Even from before the beginning there had been songs, scratched on the sides of water tanks or boxcars or among the crude anatomical drawings on jailhouse walls, nubbed out on cheap paper in missions and flophouses, passed on orally like Homer's epics around jungle campfires. The songs were often just lists of names, moniker songs that said, in effect, I was here. Sometimes they were sentimental, more often they mocked their own sentimentality or that of Victorian parlor poetry. They sang of boxcars flipped, of handouts missed and caught, of hobo utopias in the Big Rock Candy Mountains or among the fabled peaks of the Sweet Potato Range. They sang of things their singers had done, and things they wished they'd done, bluesy, insouciant, insolent, scatalogical, eschatological (visions of Hobo heavens), and almost always there was a bantering, satiric edge to them.

> Jay Gould's daughter said before she died,
> "Pappy, fix the blinds so as the bums can't ride.
> If ride they must, let 'em ride the rod,
> Let 'em put their trust in the hands of God."

The Wobblies would harness these songs, write more of their own, mold them into a coherent program of action, protest, and, ultimately, a style, a way of being. It is significant that the first great ideological battle within the newly formed I.W.W., that between the believers in an industrial course of action "at the point of production" and Daniel DeLeon's believers in a concurrent political program, was played out beyond the theological subtleties of doctrine and the power of personalities as a tale in which regeneration comes from the West in the form of J. H. Walsh's "overalls brigade." This handful of militant Wobblies had tramped their way to Chicago 2,500 miles across the country from Portland, Oregon, holding propaganda meetings and singing revolutionary songs at every stop, and their nineteen votes — and their example — were decisive in casting out the DeLeonites in the crucial I.W.W. convention of 1908. The "bum brigade" has taken over the organization, the defeated DeLeon charged. Indeed, that was just the point. No matter what the future course of I.W.W. strategy, i.w.w. dogma, i.w.w. activity, the union was actively forming itself, in its own mind and in that of the outside world, around its own version of the Western myth. By 1914, when the Wobblies had fought many of their most important battles among immigrant workers in Pennsylvania steel plants and Massachusetts and New Jersey textile mills, *Solidarity* was promoting western workers, independent, wifeless, foot-loose, nimbly hopping freights when a job turned punk, as the advance guards of the labor army, the guerrillas of the revolution.

The nomadic worker of the West embodies the very spirit of the i.w.w. His cheerful cynicism, his frank and outspoken contempt for most of the conventions of bourgeois society, including the more stringent conventions which masquerade under the name of morality, make him an admirable exemplar of the iconoclastic doctrine of revolutionary unionism. . . . His anomalous position, half industrial slave, half vagabond adventurer, leaves him infinitely less servile than his fellow worker in the East.

There was a song that was perhaps more than any other associated with such western workers. It was sung years before the i.w.w. was founded, sung by troopers in the Spanish-American War, sung by J. H. Walsh's overalls brigade, sung by Free Speech Fighters sprung from the Fresno jail, and is still being sung today. Set to the words of an old gospel tune, "Hallelujah, I'm a Bum," with its gay reversal of the grim Christian ethos of work, saving, and denial that lay under the Western myth of Owen Wister, was the essence of Wobbly style.

"Why don't you go to work
Like all the other men do?"
"How the hell we going to work
When there ain't no work to do?"

Hallelujah. I'm a bum,
Hallelujah, bum again,
Hallelujah, give us a handout
To revive us again.

In such songs the Wobblies had found their own myth and their own voice. Other labor unions might imitate the stolid virtues of the capitalist hierarchies they were trying to wring concessions from or even subvert; the Wobblies were revolutionaries in more than an economic sense. The craft distinctions that had placed skilled workers each in their jealously guarded

84

niches, scabbing on each other's strikes and guarding their doors from the unskilled, were as odious to the Wobblies as those erected between capitalist and worker. The One Big Union, which would do away with these distinctions, was more than a solution to the problem of pulling together a divided work force for more effective battle, it was a belief in something greater. The Wobblies didn't want to horn in on capitalist hierarchies; they wanted to obliterate them. "Don't worry about the bum on the rods," the song said, "Get rid of the bum on the plush." "I hope to see the day," as that exemplary Westerner I.W.W. president Bill Haywood put it, "when the man who goes *out* of the factory will be the one who will be called a scab . . . when we lock the bosses out and run the factories to suit ourselves." For the Wobblies' mission was not to found a utopia in some mental projection of the next world, but to wrench one out of history in this one. Their slogan, "One Big Union," has just this whiff of utopianism about it, and the Wobbly Father Hagerty's famous "Wheel of Fortune" diagram, with its extending spokes bearing within them all the departments of industry, could be a diagram from some latter-day Fourier.

From Marx the Wobblies got more than a description of economics and a dynamic of history; they also got a theory of consciousness. "It is not the consciousness of men that determines their existence, but, on the contrary, *their social existence determines their consciousness.*" It is a sophisticated and radical theory, in the context of its time, and one you would not imagine a union made of harvest hands, lumberjacks, and immigrant factory workers would have much interest in, but the Wobblies made it their own because they needed it. Indeed, it was the core of their belief, it was what held them together, and they used it and put it into their own words. "Listen," Red Doran said on his soapbox, "this is something you might just as well get into your head now as forty years from now. You have got to understand it sometime."

I want to give you the law of economic determination:

Man thinks in terms peculiar to the manner and condition under which he makes his living.

Given groups, thinking in like terms, create their own environment.

In order to understand the Wobbly project one has to see it as more than a battle for industrial justice, for those "porkchops" the Wobblies so disdained; one has to see it as a battle for a new understanding of the working man and woman, a new sense of self — as a battle for a new myth. Indeed, how else can you explain the faith they had? For, as I've said, they were reclaiming the privilege of making myths for the workers themselves. And what else but a new myth would allow them to pull together the most unorganizable of all the workers, what else could sustain them under the beatings, the jailings, the deportations?

4

Ultimately, that trainload of Wobblies from San Francisco made it to Denver, did their part for Free Speech. They had to. For the battle was more than tactical, more than a fight for the right to soapbox in the Slave Markets. It was a kind of rite. The mute, gray mass of men was giving itself a voice, was making its own idea of itself in its actions. One after another, in Fresno, San Diego, Aberdeen, Missoula, they came, spoke a few words, were hauled off to jail. The Wobblies themselves were amazed that they would keep coming in spite of the beatings and the torture. They found it, in its way, sort of funny. They told jokes about the stage fright of men not used to speaking in public, made up descriptions of the speakers that might have come out of vaudeville dialect skits: "Mein Fellow Vorkers! Schust you listen by me vhile I tells you somethings!" "Fellow Workers! Oi'm not much of a spaker, but Oi don't suppose Oi'll be allowed to talk long anyhow!" It wasn't even so much what they said, but that they spoke at all — that was their real eloquence. They spoke, and were slugged for it, hosed down and starved and beaten in jails, and so broken and dashed were they that the union itself began to wonder if it was worth the price, if what they were accomplishing was not destroying them in the process.

It is this split between tactics and gesture, between ideology expressed in rhetoric and ideology acted out in the world that allows us to look at the I.W.W.'s major tenets as expressions of myth. The case of sabotage gives us another example of this split between the instrumental and the mythical, for if there was one issue that placed the Wobblies at peril it was this. By refusing to give up the threat of sabotage, the I.W.W. both cut itself away from most of its erstwhile supporters on the left, and at the same time exposed itself to those civil authorities who would finally, and largely on this issue, wreck it. Again and again in I.W.W. publications one sees the symbols of the saboteur, at once ominous and gay: the wooden shoe in the cogs of the machine, the black "sab-cat" arching her sinister back, her "kitten" — the stone in the teeth of the harvesting machine, the phosphorus cake hidden in the shock of wheat – mewing for her milk. Talk sabotage they did, yet it is an open question whether the I.W.W. truly practiced it. And when its leaders came to explain it, their explanations gave sabotage not an instrumental meaning, but an ethical, almost a philosophical one. Indeed, sabotage might best be looked at as a rehearsal for the I.W.W. myth of myths, the core of its belief system, the General Strike.

Q. – Don't you think there is a lot of waste involved in the general strike in that the sufferers would be the workers in larger portion than the capitalists. . . ?

A. – The working class haven't got anything. They can't lose anything. . . . If the workers are organized (remember now, I say "if they are organized" – by that I don't mean 100 per cent, but a good strong minority), all they have to do is put their hands in their pockets and they have got the capitalist class whipped. . . . All the workers have to do is organize so that they can put their hands in their pockets; when they have got *their* hands there, the capitalists can't get theirs in.

For Bill Haywood, the one-eyed former cowboy and miner, who was the I.W.W.'s most conspicuous leader in the days before the First World War, the general strike was more than a tactic, it was an enfranchisement. It was his answer to the political program of the orthodox socialists, for it swept into its reach all those beyond the fringes of the political world, the women, children, immigrants, African Americans who had no ballot box recourse.

"I have had a dream that I have in the morning and at night and during the day," Haywood said,

and this is that there will be a new society sometime in which there will be no battle between capitalist and wage earner, but that every man will have free access to land and its resources. In that day there will be no political government, there will be no States, and Congress will not be composed of lawyers and preachers as it is now, but it will be composed of experts of the different branches of industry, who will come together for the purpose of discussing the welfare of all the people and discussing the means by which the machinery can be made the slave of the people instead of a part of the people being made the slave of machinery or the owners of machinery. I believe there will come a time when the workers will realize what the few of us are striving for and that is industrial freedom. . . . Do you know the results we are hoping for? We hope to see the day when no child will labor. We hope to see the day when all men able will work, either with brain or with muscle; we want to see the day when women will take their place as industrial units; we want to see the day when every old man and every old woman will have the assurance of at least dying in peace.

The General Strike became, in its way, a kind of prelude to the Cooperative Commonwealth, that obliteration of all class distinction, of all war, of all want. The end of history. The Big Rock Candy Mountain. Bill Haywood's dream. If history, for the workers, was the systole and diastole of job, joblessness, the anxiety of want alternating with the exactions of brutalizing work, then the end of history would be the General Strike, when the factory whistles that measured out their lives went silent. In this sense, being beyond history, the General Strike is myth. Men and women, whom the logic of mechanical production had turned into mere appendages of the wheels and levers of machines, factories and mines, anonymous "hands," would win their freedom by "putting their hands in their pockets." Their anonymity had swallowed their individual histories, their individual sufferings, had locked them into those far margins of loneliness Walter Wyckoff had described; now, in the General Strike, they would achieve their apotheosis by melting into the great felt mass of all workers, they would lose themselves, in order to merge triumphantly in the mass of men and women like themselves. In jails, on picket lines, under the brutal tutelage of those police and mine guards and detectives they called "the slugging committee of the ruling class" they had proudly answered the question "who are your leaders?" with "we are all leaders." And they were.

5

Myths, Claude Lévi-Strauss has it, are "instruments for the obliteration of time." Their function for him is essentially conservative, to forestall through their spirals of repetition the crises of the unsolvable paradoxes of biology and ideology. Yet it is just such crises as those which thrust us into the historical world. One must essentially choose between history and myth. To choose history means to choose the future, to choose the arrow of change. To choose myth means to choose stasis. Perhaps this is one way of explaining the failure of the i.w.w. to remain a powerful force in the United States. In order to exist at all they had chosen, in fact promoted, the myth. They had held out a utopia. Indeed, they had no other option. For how else were they to weld the disparate elements of their union together into one, or to organize men and women separated by language, tradition, vast reaches of territory? They looked to the lowest of the low, the most despised, the most voiceless of the workers, and they exalted them as equals to anyone. To do that, to keep them together, to keep them from collapsing under the fire hoses and sluggings and the jailings and the midnight kidnappings, they had to offer more than porkchops. They had to offer a way of being, a belief. They could not abandon their myth without abandoning who they were. Had they given up or distanced those sides of their ideology and their tactics that were most rankling to the majority of their fellow unionists and socialists, and unspeakable to the capitalists they made war upon — sabotage, the general strike, the refusal to sign time contracts, the elevation of the tramp, the African American, the immigrant — they would cease to be Wobblies. And being was what was important to them.

I have said that their myth was utopian, and surely it was. But its problem was not that it was too distant from earth, too far away in time, but that it was too close. They could not cut themselves away from the myth to ensure their survival; they could not — like that other radical sect of the frontier a generation or two before them, the Mormons — posit the most rankling of their beliefs in a dim past or a dimmer, otherworldly future. They believed too hard, the General Strike was too near at hand. Nor could they, like the communists who were to supplant them on the radical left in this country, displace their mythology into sinuosities of dogma that could be manipulated by a political elite. Because they could do none of these things, they were crushed. The myth, still vibrant, still powerful, lives on.

6

In November of 1887, while Teddy Roosevelt's cowboys were burning the Haymarket anarchists in effigy, in Chicago a transplanted Texan was congratulating himself for his part in helping to hang them. The Haymarket bombing had inspired the Texan to become a Pinkerton detective. But the words of the martyred anarchists were having a different effect on a young Nevada miner. They were to be instrumental in setting him out on a career of labor organizing that would make him the head of the most radical union this country had ever known. Forty-one years later, within a few months of each other, the lives of these two Westerners came to an end. Their careers had been at once as typical and as strange as any the West had to offer, and they will serve as emblems with which to end this chapter. Both men had been born poor boys in a West still unspanned by railroads; both of them had been cowboys, and both had drawn pistols in anger. Both had prospected and hoboed and both had mined, the elder man for a couple of months, as part of an assumed identity, the younger for more than a decade. Charlie Siringo, the elder, was the wiry little Texas cowboy who had once ridden off with seventy-five cents worth of cheap liquor and penny candy as the remains of his two-years' wages. Born to an Italian immigrant father and an Irish mother, he had gone on to a career as storekeeper, best-selling author of cowboy reminiscences, and, finally, Pinkerton detective. In that latter role Siringo had served as an undercover operative, union recording secretary, and possibly *agent provocateur* in mines in which the other man had worked and among miners that the other man would organize. Siringo's undercover work was in character, for he had probably scabbed on his fellow cowboys on the LX Ranch during their spring roundup strike of 1883.

The other man, Bill Haywood, had derived a different lesson from his cowboy experience, and had in fact once tried to organize a bronc busters' union. He had been in his day one of the best known, best loved, and most feared Westerners in America and, like Siringo, was both bearer and maker of a Western legend. Once, in an Idaho courtroom, their paths had crossed. Siringo was acting as bodyguard for his boss James McParland, whose undercover work had sent twenty-three Molly Maguires to the gallows in the 1870s, and who was now trying to do the same to the officers of the Western Federation of Miners. Haywood was one of those officers, on trial for his life.

Haywood died an exile in a Russian hospital in 1928, trapped in a revolution in which he had ceased to play any real part and which he no longer understood. Siringo's luck was better and his lifespan fourteen years longer. He outlived Haywood by seven months. He had ended up broke in Hollywood, where he spent his final days rewriting his reminiscences and acting bit parts in the horse operas which had carried the fictive world of Owen Wister and his imitators to the movie screen. By that time the corral of the LX Ranch was filled with oil wells and the old West – whatever that had been – was almost gone. Siringo didn't die famous, but he didn't die side-tracked either. He had bet on the right myth.

In the beginning all the world was America.

Locke

The Road to Oz

I

A tin man, a lion, and a scarecrow walk along a yellow road. The road winds up and down through country that is sometimes settled, but often not. At times the road almost disappears. The little girl and the dog who walk beside them are from another world of experience. Unknown to the tin man, the lion, and the scarecrow is that what they seek is who they already are; what the little girl and the dog are looking for is the way back to a place stuck in the middle of the map of America called Kansas. But all of them, those odd, animated figures, patched together from the leavings of dim nineteenth-century shops and barns, the lion drawn out of some tattered book of nursery rhymes, the girl and the dog, are going to a city made of emeralds to achieve their desires.

It is not the fairy-tale witch, her winged monkeys, the terrible Kalidahs, or any of the other menaces along the way that are the real dangers for the travelers. The real dangers are the dark possibilities that swarm up from the holes in the American project, those contradictions between our dreams and the realities out of which such dreams have been born. "It is a long journey, through a country that is sometimes pleasant and sometimes dark and terrible," the seekers are told of the way to the Emerald City. Those words might well describe the search for America itself. Being figures in a story, the Lion, Tin Woodman, Scarecrow, and girl care nothing

91

for that. They have their own troubles to think about. The dog can only sniff and bark.

..

I can not but believe, that the time is not distant, when those wild forests, trackless plains, untrodden valleys, and the unbounded ocean, will present one grand scene, of continuous improvements, universal enterprise, and unparalleled commerce: when those vast forests, shall have disappeared, before the hardy pioneer; those extensive plains, shall abound with innumerable herds, of domestic animals; those fertile valleys, shall groan under the immense weight of their abundant products: when those numerous rivers, shall teem with countless steam-boats, steam-ships, ships, barques and brigs; when the entire country, will be everywhere intersected, with turnpike roads, rail-roads and canals; and when, all the vastly numerous, and rich resources, of that now, almost unknown region, will be fully and advantageously developed. . . . And to this we may add, numerous churches, magnificent edifices, spacious colleges, and stupendous monuments and observatories, all of Grecian architecture, rearing their majestic heads, high in the aerial region, amid those towering pyramids of perpetual snow, looking down upon all the busy, bustling scenes, of tumultuous civilization, amid the eternal verdure of perennial spring . . . when genuine *republicansim,* and unsophisticated *democracy,* shall be reared up . . . where they shall forever stand forth, as enduring monuments, to the increasing wisdom of *man,* and the infinite kindness and protection, of an all-wise, and over-ruling *Providence.*

The phrases buckle in the middle, push out breathlessly. One image is scarcely proposed when another tumbles on top of it. Railroads, canals, churches, temples pile one above another. . . . It is all flackery, of course, but at a certain point that frenzied voice – it is that of the shadowy would-be empire-builder Lansford W. Hastings – pronounces a vision that rounds a bend and enters the territory of pure hallucination. In Hastings's imagined West the seasons – and with them history – are frozen into an eternal spring, Nature is prodded into an almost embarrasing fructification and all the architecture is Greek. A year after Hastings published his 1845 *The Emmigrants' Guide to Oregon and California,* the survivors of the Donner-Reed party, who had read his words and believed them, would crouch in hovels in the snows of the Sierras gnawing on each other's bones, the wreckage of their wagons and the carcasses of their cattle strewing the trail behind them from the canyons of the Wasatch to the Salt Lake Desert.

History is very thin in the American West. In some places, the leap from the Stone Age to the Nuclear Age takes place in less than a hundred years. It is this very thinness of history, perhaps, that makes the West a continuing seed-ground for utopias, which by their nature are ahistorical, remote. As the eastern edge of America becomes a kind of second Europe – settled, embedded in history, tradition, and law, the landscape of utopian possibility increasingly moves west. Cheap land, abundant resources (at least in the minds of its promotors), and the lack of established communities, laws, customs, make the American West the true utopian destination, Locke's blank slate waiting only for the bold, grandiloquent strokes of its prophets.

The West must be prepared to accept these towns and cities of the future, its harsh geography aerated, spaded, manured . . . by words. For the Frontier, imagined as the edge of somebody's map, is, after all, a mental construct. Its exaggerations and confusions are the natal broth of utopias, the amniotic juice where the past dissolves into the future and a monstrous, horrible pidgin is born. Words get unglued from their histories, float free, names peel away from their referents. *Grand scene . . . continuous improvements . . . universal enterprise. . . .* It is the discourse of ecstasy, the first squallings of the Age of Enterprise. Thus the Frontier becomes the site of some gigantic, linguistic swindle, where the worn-out glass beads and trash of European myth become the wampum of a new utopia.

So they come to the Great West, "open crowds" like the Mormons and the Wobblies, whose very existence is tied to constant expansion, a final gathering in Zion in this world and the peopling of a hierarchy of extraterrestrial heavens with saints, or the creation of the One Big Union and the General Strike; or "closed crowds" whose exclusivity secures their survival, wrapped up as they are in exotic ritual and abstruse knowledge, theosophists and the Bretheren of the New Life and that entourage of overheated Polish intellectuals who gathered around the actress Helena Modjeska on that miserable farm in Anaheim. They come and they keep on coming, the brave new communities. Ramshackle temples of Fourierists and theosophists, mystics and ecstatics, utopian socialists and followers of Étienne Cabet. They sprout from the western ground like cabbages in the night, by daylight most are tumbleweeds after all, and they blow away. In Salt Lake City the first pioneers have just begun to scratch out a few irrigation ditches to water the potatoes and corn and beans they will desperately need to fend off the first winter and already they are surveying quarter-acre lots on the desert floor and envisioning them strewn with flower plots and shade trees, imagining a temple, peaceful promenades. In that Zion – wonderful thing! – there would be communal ownership of the fruitful earth, "no land to buy and sell; no lawyers wanting to make out titles, conveyances, stamps and parchment." The voice is familiar to us, mantic, optimistic, green as grass. We already know what will become of it.

For one by one they all die. Mormonism becomes a respectable Protestant religion, the Wobblies get driven out of Goldfield by the operators and the United States Army, Madame Modjeska polishes up her English and goes back to the stage and the rest of the homesick Poles go home. Sooner or later, it happens to all of them. They break up in a smash of broken promises, false assumptions, bickerings, quarrels over deeds and titles, over water, over debts, over nothing. They catch the croup, engage in mass adulteries, burn down, blow away, run to weeds and sunflowers, get the bloody flux, get the anthrax, or get successful. They become a business, a city, a tourist trap, lapse into docility. Or they simply fade away. "A map of the world that does not include Utopia," says Oscar Wilde famously, "is not worth even glancing at, for it leaves out the one country at which Humanity is always landing." A map that doesn't include a way *out* of Utopia may be even more useless. Our sad, lost Eden, after all, is only the world, shabby since the angels have departed, leaving only us, their mincing stand-ins, parodying angelhood in fields that once were orient and immortal wheat.

Llano, Icaria, Kaweah . . . those would-be-utopias of the American West are gone for good, and someday, when on some wind-blown New Mexican mesa or among the dripping redwoods of the Mendocino coast, the last hippie crawls out of the last broken-down schoolbus and gives the final mystical sign of peace, even the idea of utopia may be gone. As for the present, what remains of most of the dreams and hopes of the western American past are only a few broken foundations, an unidentifiable hunk of rusted equipment poking out of the stinging nettles. And, naturally, words. Gazing out to the margins of what was to have been the prairie metropolis of El Dorado, Kansas, old Colonel Bywaters of Willa Cather's early story muses on such wrecks:

Often as he sat watching those barren bluffs, he wondered whether some day the whole grand delusion would not pass away, and this great West, with its cities built on borrowed capital, its business done on credit, its temporary homes, its drifting, restless population, become panic-stricken and disappear, vanish utterly and completely, as a bubble that bursts, as a dream that is done. He hated Western Kansas; and yet in a way he pitied this poor brown country, which seemed as lonely as himself and as unhappy. No one cared for it, for its soil or its rivers. Every one wanted to speculate in it. It seemed as if God himself had only made it for purposes of speculation and was tired of the deal and doing his best to get it off his hands and deed it over to the Other Party.

Humbug. Humbuggery. Somehow someone at the edge of utopia is always getting screwed.

2

THIS WAY TO THE EGRESS

Behind the glass of case No. 794: ball of hair found in the stomach of a sow; Indian collar composed of grizzly bear claws; the sword of a swordfish penetrating the side of a ship; an Algerian boarding pike; an African pocket-book; a Chinese pillow; a fragment of the first barge to reach New York through the canals; Turkish shoes; African sandals; a Mexican stirrup; a petrified piece of pork. In other cases: coach lace from George Washington's carriage; a box made of wood from the tree under which William Penn signed his treaty with the Indians; a bit of the throne of Louis XVIII; a key to the Bastille; the club that killed Captain Cook. Elsewhere in this dim, labyrinthine museum whales bump their noses against the glass of murky green tanks, boa constrictors knot themselves around branches, bands blare, automatic knitting machines stutter and click, and prize babies bawl, while on the stage dwarves posture and strut, drunkards meet their doom, and murderous Indians smoke. And up in the waxworks, between Queen Victoria and a gallery of famous criminals, Napoleon stares untwitching into the cold, dead light of the present and somewhere Jenny Lind is singing like an angel. It is as if some peddler's pack had opened to reveal all creation, now jumbled and disordered, its careful labels all unglued, its categories ruptured and leaking, its hierarchies smashed to pieces, its tuneful harmonies turned to the brash dissonance of some awful democratic howl.

Utopia hates history, history with its crush and flex, its incessant change, its brutal drumbeat of time. Utopia is all stillness, order, balance; the last place, the place where time stops. And, in its own way, time did stop at the doors of Barnum's museum. An odd sort of utopia it was, but under the chaos of the museum there lay a curious stasis in which nature and history were held at bay.

The Industrial Age is born and a profound fissure opens in the American psyche between its restless, material need for more, for the biggest, the best, and its longtime arc toward spiritual perfection. In the America of the 1840s and later, one man bridged that fissure with an ersatz utopia. Instead of history with its traps and its darkness and its vectors of force, Barnum gives us George Washington's carriage lace and his toothless old nurse mumbling hymns (and once Barnum came within an ace of buying Shakespeare's cottage). In the strange paradise he concocted, nature parodied art and art nature. The museum was a cornucopia of oddity and individuality. In its quirky corridors the iron grip of science was relaxed, gave way to the democratic liberty of quackery. The laws of nature broke down, species became unmoored from their phyla, floated free. A spine became a snake, a tree a leg. Fish sprouted wings. Everything was a category of one, everything was an exception to the rule. And what were we to make of that hideous bone-and-india-rubber fake the Feejee Mermaid? Situated on some strange, shifting margin between nature and culture, the whole category of the real dissolved, became irrelevant. The hoax became as delicious as sin – but without the consequences. And the impresario of it all was Barnum. Half shaman, half showman, like some aboriginal wizard he danced between the miraculous and the banal: canny, suggesting marvels, holding back when it suited him, even – dare it be said? – *cheating*. In his hands the wonders of the world became so much truck for his museum.

Cheerfully, cheekily, busily himself (but what self was that?) the King of Humbug never succumbed to the desire to found a colony, a sect, a party. His ambitions were more modest (he was a businessman) or perhaps more grandiose: to colonize the mind of his century. Having escaped – like a good part of his audience – from the last steely clutches of the Puritans' City on the Hill, with its ferocious repressions, its grim vision of humanity's business, he created his own ideal world in opposition – a utopia of inclusion, rather than exclusion, a nowhere that was an everywhere. Not infrequently he set that nowhere/everywhere in the fantastic treasure-house of the American West. From the fastness of the Rockies he brought back Colonel Frémont's Woolly Horse, staged a buffalo hunt in New Jersey (what matter that the buffalo were gangling juveniles?). His hoaxes were a kind of living analogue to that most Western of forms, the Tall Tale, that at once stings its audience and flatters it. Infinitely plastic, capable of dying and being reborn, of mocking itself and vaunting at the same time, the language of his public announcements became what the trickster's body was in those Indian tales – trickster that he was himself – Barnum might have enjoyed.

It was Barnum's genius to discover America's pleasure in being fooled. The pleasure we took – if it was, of course, all in fun – of being separated from our ancient beliefs, our crass inability to wonder, and from those tightly fisted coins that meant everything to the Calvinist in us. And, finally, the pleasure we took – that most terrible of all pleasures – in being separated from ourselves. Indeed, in this New World, who *was* anybody? Like the floating world of Melville's *The Confidence Man,* where, in the course of a trip down the Mississippi anyone could become anything and either everyone was everyone else, or no one was anyone at all, Barnum was all quicksilver. "Perhaps, indeed," wrote Constance Rourke, "Barnum had no personal character. In a strict sense, he had no private life. He lived in the midst of the crowd, in the peopled haunts of his great museum, on the road, on the lecture platform, on steamers, in caravans or circus trains, near the smell of sawdust or under the spreading lights of the city. He lived in public; at times it seemed he was the public."

Against the background of those stern utopias – real and imaginary – of America, all hedged about with laws, fences, hierarchies, and as many regulations as the pigeonholes of an attorney's desk, in his "dusty halls of humbug" Barnum created a Sunday afternoon utopia that suggested a world without boundaries, a world of heady, anarchic freedom. But the liberty of the museum was as dubious as the pedigree of poor old hymn-singing, psalm-mumbling Joice Heth or the Feejee Mermaid. Still, as long as the bands played and the flags flew and the American Eagle spread its wings, everything was well. And that was, perhaps, Barnum's greatest swindle of all.

3

"Where is Kansas?" asked the man, in surprise.
"I don't know," replied Dorothy, sorrowfully;
"but it is my home, and I'm sure it's somewhere."
The Wonderful Wizard of Oz

At the heart of America's dream of itself are two conflicting desires. The ancient desire – as old, perhaps, as humanity – for a just world, democratic, without hierarchy, abundant in its goodness and its gifts, and that counterdesire, more and more powerfully held since the Renaissance: a longing to place the individual at the center of the moral world.

In America these dual myths take perhaps their first, uniquely native form in J. Hector St. John Crèvecoeur's *Letters from an American Farmer,* published in 1782. In 1950, Henry Nash Smith summoned up Crèvecoeur as he traced the steps by which the classical dream of the pastoral merged with the romantic and democratic dream of the individual yeoman farmer in the American mind and marked the contradictions in their union. Like Robinson Crusoe – that good utilitarian – the yeoman farmer is a utopia of one. The farmer tends his fields, his animals, and his family; pursues happiness; and creates an island of democratic virtue in the soft lap of a pacified nature. Crèvecoeur's own pastoral idyll was disrupted by the intrusion of history in the shape of the American Revolution but the dream continued unabated throughout the European exploitation of the continent until it was stopped by the realities of geography and the rain gauge, for at last, the land itself, so yielding, so fertile in the national mind, could not support the agrarian myth.

A hundred-some years after Crèvecoeur's dream, the line of farms had straggled west into a forbidding landscape of drought and famine, plagues of grasshoppers, cyclones, mortgaged farms, and blasted hopes. For prosperity, in the American West, is cyclical: years of drought follow years of rain, boom follows bust, hope lives, and dies. By the last decade of the nineteenth century the conquistadors who first claimed this land for the Europeans had been remembered only by the names later Europeans had given to dreary little towns on the plains; the desolate prairies where Coronado and Cabeza de Vaca had found peoples living in barbarism, eating raw meat and following the herds of buffalo on foot had become the hunting grounds of the painted and mounted terrors of the West, splendid and militarized. And then the Sioux and the Cheyenne and the Apache were gone, penned up in reservations after the last protracted revolt against the encroaching whites had failed. The buffalo, too, were gone, remembered only by the wallows that still marked the plains, filled with stagnant water after summer storms. The cowboys were almost gone. The wild young men who had whooped and hollered their way through their short history were relics now, confined to fenced ranches. What remained was the land, arid, almost featureless in many places, flat as a stove lid as far as one could see. The wild fruits that reminded Coronado's homesick conquistadors of those in Spain were, it sometimes seemed, as illusory as the gold for which the Spaniards had so futilely searched. In west Kansas the rain was less than twenty inches a year, and when it came it was often in floods that broke over the cracked soil, washing out the fences and the trees that lined the muddy streams.

About the year 1890 a child stood in the doorway of a house on the west Kansas plains and looked around. What she saw was this:

Nothing but the great gray prairie on every side. Not a tree nor a house broke the broad sweep of flat country that reached the edge of the sky in all directions. The sun had baked the plowed land into a gray mass, with little cracks running through it. Even the grass was not green, for the sun had burned the tops of the long blades until they were the same gray color to be seen everywhere. Once the house had been painted, but the sun blistered the paint and the rains washed it away, and now the house was as dull and gray as everything else.

The child who looked out on that scene was a girl in a book, Dorothy Gale, the heroine of L. Frank Baum's *The Wonderful Wizard of Oz*. Thinking back on this charming, gentle tale, it is not often we remember its harsh beginning, but that beginning is crucial to understanding the world of emotional and historical experience that gave the story its birth.

The inside of this unpainted house in which Dorothy lives with her Uncle Henry and Aunt Em is as grim as the landscape without: one room, a rusty stove, a table and chairs, two beds. Bleak as this is, it is the psychological landscape that most appalls, for the sterility of the land is, in Baum's book, a version of the sterility of the souls of the inhabitants of this empty country. It represents the spiritual rubble of a shattered myth. Unsmiling Aunt Em and her voiceless husband are the bitter end of Crèvecoeur's dream, grim parodies of his vision of a nation of enlightened yeoman farmers. In them rural thrift has become an awful parsimony. Their independence is a radical alienation from friends and neighbors, almost, it seems, from society itself. The emotional desolation is terrible and poignant. The orphaned Dorothy is caught in a house without human warmth – a house, we begin to realize, without love. When she laughs her aunt can only look at her "with wonder that she could find anything to laugh at." But still Baum's Kansas was a land of dreams, as if for him dreams were the only thing left to be squeezed out of that vacant landscape. Once faith is lost – in the rain cycle, in the railroad boom, in Populism – then the land and its broken myths can only be reclaimed by turning inward, by escape to a world of fictions.

The project of *The Wonderful Wizard of Oz* was in a way to rescue its author from his own sense of failure, to incorporate that failure and re-write it. As much as any writer of fictions, L. Frank Baum was all of his characters, both heartsore Tin Woodman and brainless Scarecrow, Cowardly Lion and plucky girl. And he was also the flim-flam man at the heart of the story, the failed wizard of the city of hucksterism and illusion. After a mixed success in the East as an actor and concocter of theatrical melo-dramas, L. Frank Baum ended up in Aberdeen, South Dakota. Not so many miles north from Willa Cather's fictional Colonel Bywaters brood-ing among the ruins of the fictional El Dorado, the very real Frank Baum witnessed drought, farm failure, and the real estate bubbles that rose and burst regularly on the prairies around him. Twice failed in Aberdeen, first as a merchant, then as a newspaper publisher, in 1891 Baum moved his family to Chicago, making his living initially as a drummer for a wholesale china distributor, then, with considerably more success, as the publisher of a magazine for department store window trimmers. When, at the turn of the century, Baum came to write his second, and most famous, book for children, it was to the barren plains he had known in his days of failure that he returned. But this time he returned to rejuvenate those plains through the agency of an imaginary, supplementary world.

The cyclone that blows Dorothy Gale and her dog off the pages of this bleak Kansas prairie takes her to that world. The Land of Oz, whose name Baum got from the label of a file cabinet, is really a return to Crèvecoeur's vision: rural, fertile, filled with industrious farmers and ingenious crafts-people. The farmer-inhabitants of Oz are shrunken versions of Crè-vecoeur's yeomen, it is true, and oddly enervated, thralls as they are to both good magic and bad, but all in all, and in spite of some bad patches, this imaginary land is a good country. It is what Kansas might have been with a little luck and better weather.

But the Land of Oz is not merely a landscape of fantastic pastoral; at its heart is a city. Just as Baum himself found regeneration in a new metropolis growing up on the prairies of the Midwest, so do Dorothy and the strange companions she has picked up on her journey – Scarecrow, Tin Woodman, Cowardly Lion – come to the Emerald City to achieve their desires. City and country, strange and often threatening hinterlands and benign me-tropolis, play out theme and variation through the course of this first Oz book and all of those that were to come.

In the year 1900, the year of *Oz*'s publication, the city of the future stretched itself between two possibilities in the popular imagination. The one was summed up in a famous book by Edward Bellamy, *Looking Backward,* written in 1888. In that book, the future, peacefully surrendering to the logic of a "process of industrial evolution" has done away with the sterile getting of money, the terrible competition for success, and people live an ordered life of leisure in a technological utopia. It was a comforting vision, a seductive one, requiring of the present only a healthy optimism in the punctual arrival of a beneficent Future on the rails of technological progress. But there was a darker vision as well. The name Ignatius Donnelly is little known now, and his book *Caesar's Column,* published two years after Bellamy's utopian novel, is less read, but book and man were well known at the close of the nineteenth century. *Caesar's Column* presents a terrifying vision of the year 1988, in which the relentless logic of accumulation has widened class divisions so far that now an aristocratic oligarchy sits atop masses of people sunk in utter despair. This strange, xenophobic, death-obsessed book raises a terrifying vision of social nullity. "The truth is," writes the narrator of Donnelly's book, "that in this vast, overcrowded city, man is a drug, – a superfluity, – and I think many men and women end their lives out of an overwhelming sense of their own insignificance; – in other words, from a mere weariness of feeling that they are nothing, they become nothing." Given this nullity, many choose state-assisted suicide in special hostels. As for the rest, that great, silent mass of workers whom technology has, far from freeing, pushed into an almost medieval, serflike degradation, their end is disturbingly prophetic of the horrors of the real twentieth century.

They are whisked off, as soon as dead, a score or two at a time, and swept on iron tram-cars into furnaces heated to such intense white heat that they dissolved, crackling, even as they entered the chamber, and rose nameless gasses through the high chimney. That towering structure was the sole memorial monument of millions of them. Their graveyard was the air.

For Bellamy, the twentieth century city held out the promise of the regulated ease of technological utopia; for Donnelly, crank, xenophobe, Populist politician from the Minnesota prairies, it held the potential for revolutionary anarchy that the strikes and labor wars of his century had only faintly forewarned. If one way of seeing Populism is as the political expression of an embittered nostalgia for the pastoral idyll, it is no wonder that Donnelly would see the city as the heart of all things evil – full of corrupt luxuries and sinister foreigner-led mobs and oligarchies. Between these two visions, L. Frank Baum, ever dreaming of success, founded his own city. But his was a city planted in the untouchable reaches of wish fulfillment, and the lands of fairy tale. So, here, at last, after an arduous, miracle-filled journey Baum brought his seekers to the jewel-encrusted walls of the Emerald City. It was a city worthy of Amadis or Palmerin in the old romances, a city such as those that filled the fantastic imaginations of the conquistadors. And, indeed, like the fabulous places in Amadis's imaginary Gaul or more imaginary Greece, or the Chicago to which the bankrupt Baum turned after the failure of his Dakota enterprises, the Emerald City becomes the site of a miraculous permutation of reality into the fantastic. But now the agency of that change was not magic, but the mechanisms of modern desire.

4

The question of shop windows ∴.
To undergo the interrogation of shop windows ∴.
The exigency of the shop window ∴.
The shop window proof of the existence of the outside world ∴.

When one undergoes the examination of the shop window, one also pronounces one's own sentence. In fact, one's choice is "round trip." From the demands of the shop windows, from the inevitable response to shop windows, my choice is determined. No obstinacy, ad absurdum, of hiding the coition through a glass pane with one or many objects of the shop window. The penalty consists in cutting the pane and in feeling regret as soon as possession is consummated.
Q.E.D.   Marcel Duchamp

For L. Frank Baum, the shop windows of the new metropolis were a theater of marvels. Through their plate glass, itself a product of technological revolution, Baum glimpsed a new kind of utopia, a world of standardized goods, ready-made suits, canned foods, acres of shoes, all marching out like some great army of plenty, and like democracy, leveling taste to one common denominator. Here, in the new prairie metropolis, were the treasures of Cíbola finally achieved, and in the grasp of everyone, the fantastic obverse of the West's hard times. This was the world that Baum celebrated in his magazine *The Show Window*, a world in which desire had constantly to be stimulated by an art that was close to magic – and perhaps still closer to fraud.

"You must arouse in your audience cupidity and a longing to possess the goods you sell," Baum wrote in *The Art of Decorating Dry Goods Windows*. Yes, and the method he chose was the creation of a world of illusion behind the glass, a world of manikins and mechanical magic.

But this consumer's utopia expressed at its deepest that profound contradiction at the heart of the American project, a contradiction that, if not forced away from consciousness, could shiver the twin desires that animated the national psyche, and set them at war. In Bellamy's *Looking Backward,* Julian West finds himself thrown into a vertigo by the sight of Boston's Washington Street. He takes wondering note of the windows of the stores, watches the throngs of women looking in, and the proprietors "eagerly watching the effect of the bait." Floor walkers, clerks, all of them were bent on one task alone, inducing their customers to buy. "Buy, buy, buy, for money if they had it, for credit if they had it not, to buy what they wanted not, more than they wanted, what they could not afford."

For the fantastic fullness of the windows is a sham; beyond the glass lies a frenzy of accumulation which feeds not a utopian distribution of desire, the leveling democracy of plenty, but the rampant individualism that structures a materialistic age. The fantasy in the glass represents neither the world of Plato nor of Thomas More, but the world of Capital. The independent yeoman farmer had been replaced by his industrial bastard child, the entrepreneur, the true founder of this world of things. Indeed individualism is the name of utopia's true enemy and in Bellamy's work, it is the very thing that utopia must root out and destroy. "Individualism, which in your day was the animating idea of society," says *Looking Backward*'s Doctor Leete from his smug little podium in a twentieth century imagined by Bellamy as a social paradise, "not only was fatal to any vital sentiment of brotherhood and common interest among living men, but equally to any realization of the responsibility of the living for the generation to follow."

Baum contained in himself the paradox. Populist, Bryanite, would-be artist, he was also the epitome of the entrepreneur, showman, and merchant, writing under a handful of pseudonyms, cranking out products for a market. He solved in his fiction the paradox where, perhaps, he solved it in his life, by firmly stationing it in the realm of fantasy, a fantasy maintained by a rigorous, all-encompassing delusion. So the central figure in Oz is not some know-it-all like Bellamy's Doctor Leete, or some fiendish anarchist like Caesar Lomellini, constructing his triumphal column in commemoration of the death of modern civilization out of the bodies of the slain, but the Wizard, that balloon-borne humbug from Nebraska, who finding himself in Oz proceeds to make his section of it a utopia with the tools at his disposal. This oddly winning little confidence man, a kind of pint-sized Barnum (indeed, he had been a performer, we are told in one of the *Oz* books, in "Bailum and Barney's Consolidated Shows"), finds in a rigorous application of humbug the glue that will stick together the contradictions in Oz.

The central metaphor in this process is one that Baum adapted from the folklore of his hard days in the Dakotas. During the drought of 1890 he reported in his "Our Landlady" column that one ingenious salesman had been making the rounds of the suffering farms selling green goggles – you could put them on your mules and horses and feed them on wood shavings. Those same goggles, transported to Oz, become the green lenses through which by decree all its denizens see the Emerald City. The lie that without the spectacles one would be blinded by the brightness and glory of the Emerald City must be read in the reverse: without the spectacles, one would see only its banality. Studded with real jewels, to be sure, like the modern metropolis, the Emerald City must transform the ordinary getting and spending of the city into magic. As, indeed it does. Through the medium of the green glass, money is neutralized, is transformed, in our first view within the walls of the Emerald City, into the green pennies of children buying green lemonade. Thus the desperate commerce of the metropolis is infantalized, desire spends itself on objects oddly trivialized, made somehow safe from the psychic curse of consumption by a universal coat of green, and all we see is green candy, green popcorn, green shoes, green hats, green pennies, and green lemonade. For the penalty embedded in such material objects of desire lies in the inevitable sense of loss that goes with their appropriation. It is the genius of the Wizard of Oz that, locking the spectacles on the eyes of his subjects, the world of desire and that of the desired collapse into each other: eyes themselves become the windows of the shops. Thus to see is to possess, a constant revivifying oscillation between desire and appropriation. In the Emerald City the lie becomes the thing itself, better than the thing, in fact, for it is unarguable and inexhaustible. Its nowhere becomes the true destination. It is a world in itself, self-ratifying, complete. Entering the Emerald City is like entering the startling recesses of Barnum's museum, where the nation gapes and gawks at the freaks and wonders and finds the contradictions of the national psyche papered over by humbug and homilies.

And here the problem of individuality becomes pacified, contained. Tin Woodman, Cowardly Lion, Scarecrow, those odd companions of Dorothy Gale, become in Oz a sort of one-of-a-kind norm. "I am convinced," the Scarecrow remarks in one of the Oz books, "that the only people worthy of consideration in this world are the unusual ones. For the common folk are like the leaves of a tree, and live and die unnoticed." In a world of sham and green glasses, are Scarecrows and Tin Woodmen and Cowardly Lions – like the manikins behind the windows of the shops – more real than the deluded citizens who gaze upon them? It may have been a question that Baum, the actor and student of window dressing, might have asked about himself. Indeed, these strange, half-impotent creatures, these vivified simulacra, although they do not know it, are themselves one with their desires. Thus it only remains for the Wizard to give back to them, in the guise of a few simple symbolic puns, the heart, courage, and brains they already have. A touching moral for children, certainly, but translated to a world of adults it is as much as to say that in a land where desire can be inflamed by the cheap goods displayed behind the plate glass windows of a shop, such things are no more than labels anyway.

It is an enduring part of the fantasy of Oz that its nature is exposed when Dorothy's dog kicks over the screen behind which the Wizard, that maker of bogus magic, cowers. "I think you are a very bad man," says Dorothy to the Wizard when his true identity is revealed. "Oh, no, my dear," he replies. "I'm really a very good man; but a very bad Wizard, I must admit." But is this fraud that keeps the magic of the Emerald City intact the Wizard's imposition or his subjects' own? Like Barnum, and perhaps like Baum the salesman and prophet of the window trimmers, the Wizard has discovered, albeit a bit sadly, his subjects' incessant need to be fooled. "How can I help being a humbug," he confesses, "when all these people make me do things that everybody knows can't be done?" Is there in this sadness a hint of the disappointment that seems the inevitable aftermath of coition with the kinds of dreams promised by material desires? Those degraded proletarian masses envisioned by Donnelly had survived the grinding wheels of capitalist life, but only to be sold into a new sort of serfdom: they had become consumers, the eager purchasers of the illusions wrapped around the tawdry goods behind the plate glass windows of America's Chicagos. Their spiritual emptiness had been replaced with the never-satisfied cravings of material consumption: hope was a pair of cheap green glasses.

The potential destructiveness of these paradoxes is resolved in a way that directs Baum's stories from the realm of allegory to that of wish-fulfillment. The Wizard's humbug, his false magic and flim-flam, are replaced in the later *Oz* books by the good, maternal magic of the beautiful Ozma. It is as if sheer longing had brought her forth, and it is this unashamed longing that makes Baum's books fairy tales. Looking back, it is clear that the American pastoral could end up in no other place but where it did, in the fantasies of a failed Dakota editor set down finally in a book for boys and girls.

For Baum rarely surrendered the essential sweetness of his vision to a desire to preach. Still, in his later books, he developed the utopian nature of Oz and in so doing he relegated his works to a place that would be impregnable to both the exigencies of reality and the responsibilities of fiction. They remained fantasies, books for children. And it is just this that gives them their poignancy. The paradoxes of sexual conflict and power, which utopians had tried to solve with expedients from free love to total abstinence, and which have wrecked real and fictional utopias since Eden, were dealt with by simply banishing them from this infantile world. Individualism, strife, and issues of material property were absorbed in the benevolent rule of the eternally adolescent Ozma, who owned everything and therefore left her subjects equal in having nothing. The getting and spending, the green pennies, had entirely disappeared. The industrial army of Bellamy's *Looking Backward* (which must have given the moral willies to Baum the failed military school cadet, who knew what armies, even juvenile ones, were really like), dissolves into parody in the armies of Oz, which can muster only one private for all their officers, or General Jinjur's phalanx of girl suffragettes. For revolution, when it comes to Oz, is a matter of sweet satire, not the bloody march Ignatius Donnelly imagined it to be. When all is said and done, Oz is all much closer to *Herland* than to New Harmony or to Plato's *Republic,* and its sexual and economic solutions very like those Baum arrived at in his own life, puttering about the garden of his house in Hollywood – he called it, of course, Ozcot – and cranking out sequels to *The Wonderful Wizard of Oz;* he'd become a benign sort of Munchkin, having ceded his finances and his copyrights to the (we hope) gentle despotism of his wife. Thus it was that the Amazons the conquistadors so anxiously searched for returned to govern the New World through one of its most enduring fictions.

Utopia is a cruel place, rigid, narrow, cold, and exclusionary under its un-varying cloudless days and sunny skies, and ruled with an iron hand. For, by its nature, utopia, like the harsh despotisms of land or capital it has tried to replace, is mired in profound contradiction. Its project is, in the end, to regulate the harsh competition of men for women and property. And un-der its clear skies and carefree days it does this by means of law, hierarchy, exclusion, authority — the very tools by which men establish dominion over women and other men. Thus, to a society like our own, not held to-gether by ancient social traditions and norms, the trickster (or the trick-ster's modern avatar the humbug) is perhaps more important — and more dangerous — than to a preindustrial culture. For the Native American, the trickster represented culturally what was not; the trickster was the taboo breaker, the social failure, a figure out of whose grossness and mistakes and magic culture must be formed. For us, the latter-day Americans, the trickster represents the fluid, teasing spectacle not of what is, but what is possible. P. T. Barnum, Lansford W. Hastings, Baum's Wizard — they give us not the past, but a shifting, rainbow-hued image of a future without boundaries, without limitation. Yet such a future, conceived as without a history, is an impossibility, a dangerous dream. Indeed, what history we have, only thinly embedded in class, in social ritual, leaves us oddly vulner-able to the manipulations of humbug and the pseudo-utopias it promises. "Not only does democracy make every man forget his ancestors," Toc-queville wrote in 1835, "but it hides his descendants and separates his con-temporaries from him; it throws him back forever upon himself alone and threatens in the end to confine him entirely within the solitude of his own heart." *The solitude of one's own heart!* What crueler place could be imag-ined? What price would we not pay to escape it! Thus it is the trickster, the swindler, the humbug who rises up as our last best hope in bridging the gap between our solitude and the rest of humanity, who tries to bridge over that always-expanding chasm between the individual and utopia. But the chasm can never be bridged, the two dreams never reconciled. And this is the secret we all know about America: this terrible need to be deceived. In the Kansas of our hearts, there is one falsehood that will not die, that dream at the center of the human imagination, that home we are always searching for, that green, good place.

MX

I often imagine myself on a road. The road is always the same, a narrow track of asphalt that climbs like a thin whip through some burnt pass, then falls off, all at once, into a valley of parched sage and tufted grass, the peaks of the distant mountains floating above their roots in the mirages that fill the blank expanses with narrow sheets of illusory water. The pale sky is filled with moving armies of clouds; beyond, a far range: smoke-blue, sulfur-yellow, bone, jagged as the fossilized spine of some antediluvian creature. It is a country where all the bones show.

Even the inhabited places give no respite. You look at the map and see you are coming somewhere, and when you get there, there is nothing at all, the wind chases a few phantom tumbleweeds across the highway and there is maybe a mailbox for some ranch you can't see, a lone cottonwood, a railroad crossing with a water tank, some lineman's shack made out of an old caboose. Some of the places are bigger; first come the row of Lombardy poplars that are the sign of a Mormon settlement. Then a pasture or two, the few huddled houses and the school with its dingy flag clustered around the Ward House. Other places seem to have no meaning, stuck randomly in the middle of the desert: you stop to get something to drink in one of those dusty little stores that are nothing but a cooler full of beer and soda pop and you wonder how this settlement has come to be. Then you drive around a bend and see the beards of overburden spilling down a ravine stained rust or copper green, a hole in a slope like a badger might dig, maybe a rusted-out ore car, a piece of twisted track. Sometimes you leave the main road and come to the remains of some boom town no longer on the map, no trace left of the crowded streets, the stained canvas tents, the jerry-built saloons and whorehouses and Chinese hop joints, only the gigantic concrete foundations of the mills and crushers, the stumps of a headframe or the entrance to a mine, and the local people will tell you of the pockets of silver or gold still folded into the slopes, the reservoirs of wealth only waiting for the right technology, the right market, the right time; of other minerals whose names are as exotic as their uses – lithium and beryllium and gadolinium. They live off such bones out here. Driving off you think only of how thin the line of civilization – or what passes for civilization in these dusty little oases – really is. And then it is the desert once more. You look on the map and know exactly where you are, yet you are always lost in a vastness that replicates the vastness out of which you came and the vastness over the next spine of hills. It is a landscape of a sort of waking nightmare of recurrence, of awful, unmediated space.

And always in my mind there are the fluttering lines of yellow ribbons plotting out the arid valleys and talus-skirts of the slopes. And the dust. For this place exists in my imagination as it once was dreamed by scientists and generals and engineers and political leaders and the bureaucrats they led and were led by, as the site of a great military arsenal, a weapons system that would, when it was built, become a project greater than the Panama and Suez canals, greater than the pyramids or the trans-Siberian railway. And so I imagine the dust. At first it is barely visible, a thin haze beneath the mountains, a faint moving line. Then it stretches out like a band of yellow-gray smoke across the far valley. When you get nearer the smoke begins to break up, it looms across the road dense and blowing, tufting in rooster tails from the earth-moving equipment. The dust is always there, powdering trucks and cars and the windows of buildings, lodging in the creases of peoples' skins, in the delicate lines of the faces of the children, caught in the seams of clothing, the stitching of shoes. In some places the dust is visible for 300 miles.

Is it really impossible to touch gambling without
immediately becoming infected with superstition?
Dostoyevsky

There was a story that could not be told in our world. It existed, sometimes dimly glimpsed through dry rows of figures and the abstractions of graphs, sometimes poured out as improbably as in any soap opera or the doom-laden visions of electronic evangelists, or stuttered into our ears in an embarrassed aside. It was the story of the end of the world. The story could not be told because it could never be fully imagined. For even when it was put forth with clarity and boldness, as it came to be with increasing frequency in the last decades of the twentieth century, it remained a self-annulling projection into the future of a tale that was an impossibility. Who would be left to tell it? Or to whom? Or who could even think it in imaginations once so adept at making alternative worlds of experience, corrections to this one? But here there was no alternative world to which we could appeal: the small chambers of the imagination, like the secret rooms only children know, collapsed beneath the impossibility. In our attempts to comprehend the end we were as impotent as Archimedes, who boasted that he could have moved the world if he'd had a place to stand. For where was the ground on which we could place the levers of an imagination that must be able to comprehend its own destruction, and that of everything else?

On 5 March 1946, the Cold War began. A historian might mark the beginning with Potsdam or Yalta or with the movement of some triumphant army into one or another liberated city in Europe, or at any other point where force and policy began to decide the destiny of the postwar world. But it was on that March date in 1946, seven months after an atom bomb had obliterated Hiroshima, that Winston Churchill made the speech that gave to the Cold War the rhetorical dimensions that were to constrain the way people would think about their lives for almost the next half century. Speaking at Westminster College, in Fulton, Missouri, Churchill created a mythology that will continue to haunt our thinking and shape our decisions into the twenty-first century, beyond the toppling of the Berlin Wall, the independence of central Europe, the break-up of the Warsaw Pact and of the Soviet Union itself.

The title Churchill gave to his address was "The Sinews of Peace." It is an interesting speech, full of the basest sort of flattery to Churchill's host country, full of sentimentality, of cunning and melodrama, of half truths and Anglo-Saxon chauvinism, extending on the one hand a mawkish vision of the United Nations as utopia, fostering peace on every side, protector of wage earner and cottager, and on the other hand of Armageddon. In a curious way – or are there only a few stories in the world after all? – the speech hauntingly parallels the Shoshonean myth of technology and human destiny, the Theft of Fire. The elements of the myth embedded in Churchill's speech are these:

A Secret

A Race

A Curtain and a Game

A Blessing and a Curse

Like fire, nuclear fission is a secret, jealously guarded by its owners, furiously sought by those who lack it. When Truman announced the dropping of the atom bomb on Hiroshima he called this secret "a harnessing of the basic power of the universe" and stated that it was not to be divulged in its full outlines for strategic reasons. Churchill raises the holding of the secret to a mystique. One that magically empowers its possessor. No matter what its military value, no matter what its danger, possession of the secret of the bomb in itself confers an aura of potency on its holder. And, at first, an aura of spiritual election as well. For God had willed that the plan of the bomb had not first fallen into the hands of some communist or neofascist state. Thus the secret had been the end-point of a race – a race for knowledge. Allied scientists, each building on the work of the others, pried the secret out of the atom, just as the birds in the Shoshonean myth push higher and higher in their effort to sight fire. Truman had called this phase in the bomb's development "the battle of the laboratories," the race against the Nazi scientists for the secret of the bomb. By the time of Churchill's Fulton speech the idea was more fully worked out. If the secret cannot be held by its possessors indefinitely, nonetheless, if no effort were spared, the Allies "should still possess so formidable a superiority as to impose effective deterrents upon its employment, or threat of employment, by others." The thought is extended into a utopian future: when the United Nations can truly express the essential brotherhood of humanity, the secret of nuclear fission – "with all the necessary practical safeguards to make it effective" – would be confided to the world organization.

It is, of course, a future that would never come. For the race itself, now seen as a race for nuclear superiority, is stamped as an image on the language that contains it, is self-perpetuating: a race without a goal and without an end. Having created the terms of the race, we feel impelled to uphold them.

In part, what ensures the continuance of the race is Churchill's most memorable metaphor, a metaphor that soon ceased to be a rhetorical trope and generated a politics of its own, and this is the image of the Iron Curtain. The reality behind that image, Stalin's politics of Gulag and Commissar, is not the issue. The issue is the metaphor itself and the point at which it ceases to attempt to describe reality and usurps the function of that reality in its own right. In the world of the savage, for all the strangeness of its ritual and the pervasiveness of myth, it is reality that, ultimately, sanctions myth; with Churchill's speech we have fully entered the age of propaganda. Now it is rhetoric that sanctions reality.

With the coming of the Cold War and the thermonuclear weapons that were its mystified armaments, came a new sense of strategy, a whole new way of thinking about war. Now military success would be for the first time measured by battles that would not be fought, armaments would be piled up for a war whose total destruction could not be permitted, and hence must exist only in the mind. Daily, in the war rooms, in the military colleges and think tanks, battles were being waged on computer screens and in payoff matrixes that would have to stand for those that must never begin. It was a war not for an inch of territory or a pound of tribute, but a shadow war, and its purpose was pure terrorism.

The coming of the Cold War and its weapons brought as well a new language, a new way of ordering strategic thought. It was a language of *Gedanken* experiments and "scenarios." Since the war was, after all, a thing of the mind, in a very real way the battle was not so much with the Soviets as with the home guard, the average men and women who would have to buy the assumptions of the planners and politicians and vote the immense sums of money necessary to maintain and procure the new weapons systems, the bombs and bomber planes, the arsenals of ever new missiles that were always on the verge of obsolescence even as they were finally being deployed. And because the war was a thing of the mind, its object was, in a large measure, linguistic; a battle to control the rhetoric of war, to create the metaphors by which it could be understood and justified. If it produced vast arrays of hardware, trip wires of radar scanners at the DEW line, ever more powerful missiles, bombers, and tactical nuclear weapons, ever more sophisticated computers to manage the incredible amount of information necessary to process the blips that showed on radar screens, the trajectories of missiles, and the calculations of strategists, these were things that were glimpsed only rarely, if at all, on the screens of our television sets. The sites where the battles would be planned and fought were unavailable. No one had been to the war room in the Pentagon or to the depths of Cheyenne Mountain; the Command and Control centers were as remote as the inner chambers of the Jade Emperor's palace.

What remained constantly before us, in forms both popular and debased, and in the serious think pieces of journals and newspapers, were the words. The war had become a literature. We were asked on the one hand to participate in the mythology that Churchill had laid out in the Iron Curtain speech, while on the other we were invited to imagine how the unthinkable, the use of atomic weapons, might actually become thinkable, even inevitable amid the tensions of the Cold War.

The military expression of this terror was a doctrine of defense that came to be known by its acronym MAD, or Mutual Assured Destruction. Technically, the doctrine was really that our forces and those of the Soviets had an assured *capability* for mutual destruction. It was a distinction that gave little comfort to the squeamish, who saw whole populations now held hostage under a threat of impossible terror. The idea of MAD was just that, to so build up armaments on both sides of the Curtain that no one would be foolish enough to use them. There would be such redundancy that even after a surprise attack retaliation would be as terrifying to contemplate as suffering a first strike. It was within this curious nonplace of deadly parity, this land of negatives, in which both sides played only for stalemate, that the nuclear game, so strangely detached from its consequences, so aesthetically formalized, would be worked out until 1972.

The historian and activist E. P. Thompson used a term to describe our relationship to this gamble of Mutually Assured Destruction. The term has since become somewhat shop-worn with overuse, but in Thompson's application to the strategy of deterrence that molded our defense posture and our common psyche for three decades it has a chilling accuracy. He called it an addiction. Like the addict, we fed on the drug that was destroying us, the very fear that it was to have warded off became increased with our need for the drug itself: we were poisoning ourselves with it. The addict of deterrence was a gambler too, but unlike the addict gambler, the addict of deterrence was without hope. The gambler was after all banking always on that one big win, the one final pot that would wipe out his losses; it was just this showdown that the addict of deterrence most feared. His only wish was to prolong a game he knew could not be won.

3

The system *is a body of doctrine within which the elements (principles, facts, consequences) develop logically. . . . it is a strictly paranoid insanity whose path of transmission is insistence, repetition, catechism, orthodoxy.* Roland Barthes

The problem was with the treaties. Since the atmospheric test ban treaty in 1963, the treaties that had constrained our testing and procurement of weapons had in fact become a part of the weapons systems themselves, built into their design. That first treaty had only dealt with the present and measurable danger inherent in the weapons' development – the very real poisoning of the atmosphere by their testing – not with the dangerous potential for their use. Like subsequent treaties its effect was not to curtail the building of new weapons systems, but instead to raise the level of technology necessary to develop and test them. It was as if new rules had been imposed whose function was not to abolish the nuclear game, but to make it more difficult, its solutions more elegant and fabulous.

In 1972, the United States and the Soviets agreed to a major statement of principle in SALT (Strategic Arms Limitation Treaty) I. By rigorously limiting the number of antiballistic missile rockets, or ABMs, the great powers confirmed the doctrine of deterrence that was in place. For without substantial arsenals of missiles targeted to destroy other missiles, both nations held their populations open to attack. The temptation to launch a massive first strike would be tempered by the sobering thought of the massive counterattack that would be the response. An attack for which there would be no defense.

But technological development had not stopped. Missile silos had become hardened to withstand enemy attack, missiles themselves had become heavier to break these hardened silos. Moreover, a disturbing new development had occurred in conjunction with the development of the

ABM systems. That was the program of arming our missiles with not one but as many as fourteen separate warheads, the system of multiple independently targetable reentry vehicles, or MIRVs. Now technology had provided a new and unsettling element to the standoff. When single-warhead missiles were matched against each other, a first strike made little sense. There would always be failures, missiles that didn't hit their targets, failed on launch, failed to detonate. The failures would always leave a balance on the side of the defenders. Multiple warheads made this theory obsolete. One missile might destroy several enemy missiles with its warheads. The balance would be on the side of the attackers.

SALT II, signed in Vienna on 18 June 1979 by the United States and the Soviets, was the most current of the treaties. Against these threatening new developments of MIRVs, heavier, silo-busting missiles, and other perceived imbalances, as well as new weapons such as the radar-evading cruise missiles, SALT II attempted to impose limitations. Even so, SALT II was going too far for powerful elements of Congress and the military establishment. So alongside SALT II came a new missile from the Pentagon drawing boards, and a new way of basing it. By 7 September 1979 the Carter administration had decided to go ahead with both the weapon and the basing plan. The weapon was the Missile Experimental.

It was a weapon no one much wanted. It served no real military purpose; moreover, it was dangerously destabilizing. The MX, as it came to be called, was in itself fearful, twenty-four times more powerful than any missile in our arsenal, tipped with ten to twelve independently targetable warheads, each a hydrogen bomb thirty-five times more powerful than the bomb dropped on Hiroshima, and able to pierce the hardened silos of the enemy force. Embedded in the design of the MX was a new theory of defense, one that moved beyond the old idea of a balance of terror. Where once the mighty nations had lived on the brink of mutual annihilation, in a parity of mistrust, now that balance was perceived as unstable, the arsenals of rockets and warheads were vulnerable to each other, the systems themselves could be destroyed. And so, it was argued, a new generation of weapons was needed, weapons capable of a first strike. Immense, powerful, swift, able to smash through the concrete and steel silos protecting the missiles of the other side. But these missiles must be invulnerable themselves, they must be hidden.

It was the basing of the missiles, then, that was the chief difficulty. For they must be both mobile and, in the curious scholasticism of the arms ne-

gotiations rituals – those ghostly glosses on the weapons systems themselves – available to the observation of the Soviet satellites: the missiles had
to be both hidden and open at once. There were different solutions to the
launching problem. At first the idea was to hide the missiles in trenches, to
run them in underground tunnels on tracks and only on launch to open the
ports in order to fire them. Or perhaps they could be simply hidden in boxcars, disguised like any of the other cars on the tracks and shunted to the
civilian rail circuit in time of an alert. Or they could be mounted on
trucks. . . . For a couple of strange months the idea of basing them in a fleet
of dirigibles made out of the stuff used for bullet-proof vests was even studied. But there were obvious problems. A blast at one end of a tunnel would
run its length, twist the rails, disable the whole system. And the thought of
nuclear-tipped missiles parked on railroad sidings next to peaceful boxcars
or being trucked down the interstate highways was not only frightening,
but politically disastrous. There was another solution.

The theory was a simple one. In the remote valleys of the Great Basin,
where the land was both flat enough and empty enough to make it possible, there would be laid out miles of road in looping tracks, with shelters
along that road to house the missiles and hide them from enemy observation. Missile transporters would drive from shelter to shelter, depositing
their cargo. The enemy, watching from his satellites, would never know if
the transporter crawling along the desert floor had deposited in the shelter
the launcher and half-million-pound missile with its lethal warheads or the
dummy missile and launcher it also carried. The enemy would never be
able to target and destroy all the shelters; the desert would absorb his arsenal like an immense sponge. From time to time, as required by SALT II, the
ports in the shelters would be opened to the sky, and to the spying eyes of
the Soviet satellites.

It was a gamble based on what you thought you saw, what you guessed.
What the theorists called a game of "imperfect information," like poker or
the old handgame of which the Indians of the desert had been so fond.
When plans for the system began to appear in journals and newspapers,
with the first drawings of the looping roads, the shelters, the immense
transporters, it seemed almost impossible to believe, as impossible as even
the preliminary figures of dollars attached to it. The missile, its launcher,
transporter, and shield would weigh more than one and a half million
pounds. There would be 4,600 concrete shelters, clustered in groups of 23
along a network of roads like grapes on a stem, enough to ensure the sur-

vival of half of the missiles, even if the system were attacked by all of the Soviet arsenal allowed by SALT II. There would be 9,000 miles of roads. The entire system would spread over 40,000 square miles, a territory as large as Michigan. Its construction would absorb 40 percent of the nation's cement production for three years.

The drawings that began to appear in newspapers and journals testified to the magnitude of the project. Vast tracts of western Utah and apparently most of southern Nevada would be taken up by the system, its ancillary support bases, and control centers. It was a sobering thing to see it laid out this way, mapped, visible. But in fact, the system had always been there, and now we knew it. It had been implicit in our defense theories all the time, in the complex linkage of ideas and strategies and government committees and in the minds of military and civilian planners, of senators and defense contractors, in the computer simulations and the payoff matrixes in the think tanks and war rooms, in the industries that served the military and were served by it; it had been embedded all the time in our fears. Only we had never seen it, never known it. When President Jimmy Carter first got a look at the plans, he is said to have remarked that it was the craziest thing he had ever seen. Months later he was bending the immense resources of his office to implement it.

Decision by decision the missile came closer to becoming a reality. It passed through committees, through review processes, always compromised, constrained, a bad solution its negotiators were willing to live with. Or perhaps to die with. You think of the medieval cathedral, that collection of abstruse theology, platonic mystery, pagan superstition, and scholastic numerology, all made manifest in stone and glass. The cathedral pointed upward, away from a lost and hollow world to some loftier alternative; the system on the desert pointed nowhere but to that other immense network of silos and radar antennae and command centers which replicated it on the other side of the globe. And if the medieval cathedral contained within itself a view of humanity as lost and sinful, it also saw it as ultimately savable. The view of humanity contained in the MX was different. In its nihilistic description the human animal was a cunning, frightened being, full of bellicosity and bluff, and, finally, without hope. We were creatures without vision who could only buy our days on earth a pinch at a time, forestalling doom in little increments of stalemate, creatures of despair. The miles of looped roadway connecting the MX system were a kind of negative utopia, a refuge from history and from reality itself, wrapped in obsessive layers of computer simulation and strategic doctrine.

And the weapons system was more abstract than any cathedral could ever be. Because beyond the incense and the mystery, the cathedral worked. Somehow all that arcane wisdom translated itself into buttresses that carried the weight of real walls, arches that held fast, windows that caught the light. But no one would ever know if that million-and-a-half-pound maze of formulas and Cold War dogma and computer chips and steel and bits of fissionable matter crawling along on the configuration of roads leading nowhere out on the desert would work or not. Its justification was that it would not have to. It was just as well. The system would have a lifespan of twenty to thirty years. It would be obsolete before it was finished.

..

So, shaped by our most advanced technology and bent according to the limitations of our arms negotiations, the system stood, built on a treaty that had not even been ratified by our Congress. And if SALT II were not ratified? If SALT II's limitations did not hold, if the Soviet's broke out? The system would still work, it would grow to absorb more and more of the Soviet missiles, their numbers not capped by any law save their willingness to build. "We can maintain our deterrence by deploying more shelters," said a Department of Defense undersecretary. "We can build shelters at a rate of two thousand per year. We could have, for example, a ten thousand shelter system completely deployed by 1989." It was what the gamblers around the tables in Las Vegas called "chasing": risking more and more in the hope that your debt to the game would be wiped out.

4

On maps it was a sparsely populated place. There were no cities, only a few towns, most of them little more than settlements. There were a few farmers, a few ranchers and miners, a few Indians. There were minerals there, grazing cattle, herds of sheep, but on those flattened paper landscapes dotted with little flecks of population or the shadings representing annual housing starts or industrial production or per capita income or fast-food franchises or air pollution or televisions per household or almost any of those late-twentieth-century ways of measuring a civilization, the land was empty. In the minds of the planners the vast desert of the Great

Basin was ideal – ideal as a site for the system that would serve as a great deception, a monstrous shell game played over millions of acres of desolate land.

It was, after all, not a new idea, this vision of the empty landscape as the stage for the most advanced and secret military tests. It was here, during the last months of World War II, that the first atomic bombs were assembled. These same desolate valleys had been used later for the atmospheric testing of nuclear weapons whose clouds of radioactive dust had blown across vast tracts of land, poisoning towns from southern Utah to the Dakotas and unsuspecting soldiers who were sent out with little more than dark glasses to protect them from dangers that were yet unrealized. The maps of the desert were still marked off with huge tracts labeled *test range, no public access.* It was part of a perception that saw the deserts of the American West as unredeemable, a kind of immense sinkhole on the map, and the fit repository of the leavings of a culture of waste.

The story was an old one and it went back beyond the vast and ominous stretches of territory marked off as the Great American Desert in nineteenth-century atlases, went back as far as those Puritans who saw the unexplored place west of the cornfields and the blue smoke of the settlements as Satan's Den, the haunt of hellish fiends who "devils worshipped." The vision of the West as a place of renewal and regeneration had alternated with that of the West as the dark side of the American soul; now, quite literally, those vast spaces of the Great Basin were to house the most technologically advanced expression of our fears. So the immense system that was now proposed was only an extension of this logic, the billions of dollars, the untold hours of human effort that would be thrown into a weapons system whose intention was that it never be used was only a continuation of the past. In one of the unhappy phrases that would haunt this project, MX apologists began referring to the Great Basin as a "national sacrifice area." The assumption being that it was someone else's sacrifice, someone else's backyard that was being turned into a gigantic target to absorb the initial hits of the Soviet nuclear arsenal. Two years before the first briefings of state officials, Air Force geologists had already begun taking core samples from areas of the Utah-Nevada border.

The country that this system was to be planted upon is on the whole a conservative one. There is a tradition of individual effort, bred by the independence of isolated ranchers and miners. And there is a distrust of social solutions proposed by distant academics, a public image of self-reliance.

The Mormon Church, whose paradox is that it couples a commitment to an efficient welfare system within its confines with a rigid suspicion of liberal causes beyond them, is also an important source of this conservatism. Yet in fact – and this in turn may be a part of its psychology, a knowledge suppressed, defended against – the Great Basin is a dependent region as well. Dependent on huge federal power and irrigation projects, on grazing rights and mineral leases on the public lands that make up so much of its territory; dependent for employment on the military installations taking up huge areas of its map, on the federal highways that are its lifelines, on railroads originally built out of grants of land and money and infusions of graft skimmed from the public purse, on Eastern money. So it was that the coming of the MX was first accepted, if not welcomed, to the area by some of the same politicians and institutional leaders who would later turn against it.

Ten years earlier, fifteen, in the early 1960s, say, and the system might have been put in place, with the generation after it left to wonder at its use. But at the time the mobile basing plan was being introduced in the late 1970s, the Great Basin was experiencing a strange political movement, half-populist, half-swindle, called the Sagebrush Rebellion, an attempt to win back federal land for the states of Utah and Nevada. And then there was another development; namely, the introduction of a public literature which by law was an integral part of the MX basing process, and which no doubt will one day be almost all that remains of the system in public archives.

This literature was a new addition to public life in this country: the Environmental Impact Statement, or EIS in the terminology of the bureaucrats. The National Environmental Policy Act of 1969 had mandated the study of the effects of major federal legislation on the "productive harmony" between humans and nature. The whole concept of such a work – the idea of public hearings, public surveys, and impact statements – was foreign to this part of the West, as demonstrated by the denuded slopes around the Comstock Lode, where whole forests had been cut down to provide firewood for the tent cities of miners and charcoal for primitive reduction plants, by the mercury-poisoned streams around the gold fields, by the tractored-up piñon pine groves cleared for grazing, and by, of course, those clouds of nuclear dust. The Indians had known the fragility of the land. It was something the whites had never learned, but now were having to learn, and learn in their own way.

And so the contracts were let. Consulting groups were hired to prepare reports on the effects of the missile system on every aspect of the environment, on the archaeological remains of the primitive inhabitants, on the flora and fauna, on the geology, on the ranchers and laborers and shopkeepers and the little towns they inhabited and their way of life, on the Native Americans on and off the reservations. The conclusions of the draft Environmental Impact Statement were not encouraging.

But there were to be benefits. The very building of the system would create a wealth of possibilities. In his essay on the MX Edward Abbey collected a rare bit of flackery in the form of a Pentagon brochure:

MX will present new business opportunities for companies during construction and operation. . . . New business will in turn stimulate new job and career opportunities. Some – such as administration, fire protection, security, clerical, construction and maintenance – will result directly from the construction and base operation. Many other jobs will arise indirectly as a result of construction and permanent area growth. Payroll dollars from the construction workers and permanent base personnel will be spent on restaurants, cars, new homes, clothing and other consumer goods. This will build up the capital in local banks available for loans, boost collections of state and local taxes, and help to maintain the stability of the communities for the future.

The line about "stability" is interesting, given that the beneficiaries of all this largess would be sitting in the midst of the greatest nuclear target on the earth – but what is more to the point, what the quote is really about is the boom or bust mentality that is an old story in the West.

I have a nightmare about the desolate road of my imagination. Now the road is full of trucks and semitrailers and the four-wheel-drive vehicles of the surveyors and engineers. There are long pile-ups of big rigs and pickups with mushroom clouds and "use it or lose it" bumper stickers on the interstates. At Reno and Las Vegas and even in isolated places like Beryl and Coyote Springs, the valleys kick up brown tatters of smog. The most remote ranch and mine roads have plumes of dust rising above them, and the drilling rigs sucking up the hundred billion gallons of water needed for the concrete batch plants dot every valley floor. Eighteen-wheelers carry steel girders, well-drilling outfits, prestressed concrete beams, immense sheaves of reinforcing iron like the trunks of redwoods. Huge, severed signs announcing the businesses that will serve the new settlements of airmen and hardhats and engineers move by on their sides like trophies of a war, Dinosaurs and Cowboys and immense spurting Missiles and Cocktail Glasses and clinking Dice. Night and day, preceded by the lead cars with their warning lights, the open shells of prefab houses pass by, an eerie spectacle of bisected living rooms and kitchens like sets for some transient sit-com waiting for its actors. It is as if a whole civilization has suddenly picked up and packed itself off for some ghostly migration through the desert.

There is a little town in southeastern Nevada called Caliente. It had been the site of an isolated cattle ranch and a division point for the rail line between Salt Lake and Los Angeles, and had lapsed, with the removal of the roundhouse and shops into a quiet hamlet of fewer than a thousand people. It had a dry goods store, a bank, a few grocery and hardware stores, a car dealer, a few motels and cafés, and four bars. The people of Caliente ranched, worked on the railroad and at the Nevada State Girls' Training School, in the Bureau of Land Management office, and for the Soil Conservation Service. Just over the range of mountains west of Caliente, in Dry Lake Valley, was the site of the first MX missile clusters. In 1981 the people of Caliente were worried about what effect the missile would have on their lives.

It was the kind of place, people claimed, where most of the residents had forgotten where they had put the keys to their front doors. It was also divided in various ways, between Mormon and non-Mormon, between retired people and the young businessmen who ran the few stores and services, between denizens of the four bars and those who spent their nights at home. With the coming of the MX the population of the town would double in the first year, and might go as high as 5,500 people. There would be new jobs, an influx of money which most of the people of the town claimed was desperately needed. But there would also be problems whose magnitude no one could finally predict, with hordes of new people entering the narrow valley where the town was located, burdening schools, services, scarce supplies of water, and available building land. Caliente, with its railroad tracks cutting the town in half, its dreary line of shops and services, was a typically bleak western hamlet. But it was a real place, too, and people knew each other and liked the town. With the MX it would become, some said, a sprawl of trailers and fast-food franchises and bars — and of crime, and drugs. The people who had settled in Caliente had seen boom towns before, in Alaska along the pipeline, in California. They knew what had happened to Tonopah, 160 miles to the west. And they worried about what would happen when it all collapsed, when the construction workers hooked up their trailers to their pickups and packed up their dirt bikes and went on to the next boom town. The MX, as an idea, as something not yet accomplished, became a kind of test in Caliente, and the thoughts of the people meeting each other in the post office or at the Mormon Ward House or in the bars were expressions of both western xenophobia and of that western optimism that had come with the territory and that had built, out of little more than sagebrush and dust, towns such as Caliente itself had once been.

One afternoon, in the college auditorium at Cedar City, Utah, 100 miles east of Caliente, 200 people gathered to listen to a series of experts testify on the MX and to watch the slides that were part of the Air Force's hearings on the draft Environmental Impact Statement. But experts were not the only ones who testified that day. The residents of the towns and hamlets and isolated ranches of the Utah-Nevada border spoke as well. To the military men and planners who saw the issue in terms of the jargon of global strategy, their voices must have been strangely personal and direct, and many of them opposed the missiles. A rancher's daughter got up and read from a prepared statement. She spoke nervously, stopped to steady her voice, went on. "You know just how to make the people of this area feel important," she said.

You need our housing. You need our local services. . . . You need our land, you need our water, but you don't know exactly how much. You, in fact, need everything we have. . . . Today you come to us with your draft environmental impact statement and request us to give you our life. This is our reply: we will not sell our birthright for a mess of pottage. We are an honest, industrious, independent people. We don't need your temporary jobs.

Others stood to speak. Another woman told how most of them – their families – had come out in the early days and that life was hard. "We came from good, tough people and we aren't afraid of anything," she said, "but we really don't like MX." A man spoke of freedom: "We're one of the last frontiers in the West where we have wide open spaces and the freedom to go and come as we please and to see the out-doors as we've enjoyed it all our life. I'd just hate to see it destroyed."

In Battle Mountain, in northern Nevada, a reporter for National Public Radio sat at a table with a group of Shoshone Indians. Even before the MX, two Shoshone women had challenged the U.S. claims to the public lands of Nevada, arguing that the Shoshones had never ceded this land, had never

124

been compensated for it. The Indians in Battle Mountain saw the withdrawal of land for the missile system as part of the same pattern of dispossession.

"If the MX [comes] within that area, then we're excluded from doing these things we've been doing for hundreds of years," a man said. "It's gonna be complete destruction of everything," a woman put in. Another man spoke: "If the atmosphere's disturbed, if the mother earth's disturbed in any portion, in any way, then it destroys the circle of life – the mother feeds the children and the children are the Indian people. And everything within that mother, if it's destroyed by whatever, you have nothing, you have no children."

The reporter asked if there were a phrase in Shoshone to describe MX. One of them spoke, then translated: "It's a bad thing that the white people have brought here."

The issues of who the people of the Great Basin were and what they would become were not easily squeezed into the plans for the missile, into its range of measurements for social degradations and what in the language of the social planners who followed as a horde upon the military planners were called "offsets" or "mitigations." Scott Matheson, the governor of Utah, looked at the Air Force's draft Environmental Impact Statement and noted that thirty-one pages were devoted to the pronghorn antelope, seventeen to rare plants, twelve to the sage grouse, and five and one half to the effect on human beings. In Las Vegas they were not worried about the degradation of anyone's life. Patriotic realtors had formed something called Citizens for a Strong National Defense and were promoting their views in the "MX Business Opportunity Newsletter." Plans were being broached for a high-speed train to run gamblers and construction workers back and forth between Las Vegas and the Coyote Springs base to check out each other's action.

5

A toss of the dice will never abolish chance. Mallarmé

It is always dangerous to gamble the last thing. Caught up in the excitement of gaming, the gambler forgets that there is a world outside; he forgets that the value of what he wagers is found only beyond the margins of the game, in things that are fine and useful and to be preserved. But he forgets all that. He wagers his wildcatskin quiver, his arrows, and his bow. He wagers his blankets and his clothes and sits there naked. He wagers his wives and children and loses them. Finally, he loses even himself.

Centipede was a great gambler who played the handgame and football. Men and women would leave their homes in the valley to play with Centipede, and none came back. Finally only two girls and a boy were left of all the tribe. The boy grew up, learned to hunt. One day he caught a little bird. The bird said that if the boy would spare him he would make a great man of him. He told the boy that far across the mountain lived a bad man who had killed all the people and cut out their hearts and hands to hang in his lodge as trophies. The bird gave the boy two magic eggs which would hatch two birds who would fly him to Centipede's house. He told the boy that in the morning Centipede practiced the handgame. When the boy flew over him he was to spit on Centipede's head. By no means was he to sit on the red robe Centipede would spread for him, nor was he to play the handgame.

When the boy awoke the next morning he was a handsome man. He flew to Centipede's lair with the help of the birds hatched from the magic eggs. He did not play the handgame with Centipede, but instead played a game of football. With the aid of Owl, who with his blinking eyes saw the boy's ball in the dark tunnel in which they played, and Gopher, who dug a hole that Centipede's ball disappeared into, the boy beat Centipede at his game. The boy refused the offer of the hearts and hands of the dead men and women, as he had been instructed, but with Crow's help seized Centipede himself as his prize and threw him into the fire. Then the boy set off, burying the dried hearts and hands in a damp place every night. On the third night he came home, and in the morning, while he pretended to sleep, his sisters heard laughter and conversation. It was their parents and other relatives revived. The boy had won back the dead.

The people in the Shoshone tale had lost their lives gambling with an ogre whose magic was stronger than their own, hundred-handed Centipede. We were gambling too, with the missiles. And where was the magic that would save us?

That magic was in technology itself, technology that had so removed itself from our everyday experience that it was capable, we believed, of accomplishing anything. Technology itself would provide our shield, our protection. And it would be the road to a new civilization. It was a fantasy, the ancient wish for a charm that would lead us back to Eden, to the place where life was easy and without fear, to a place beyond the burdens of our own humanity.

126

In Winston Churchill's mind, as he spoke at Fulton, Missouri, in the middle of the twentieth century, there was no doubt that science and cooperation could soon bring to the world "an expansion of material well-being beyond anything that has yet occurred in human experience." It was the dream of a technology that could conquer want and death. But in Churchill's next breath came the threat: "The dark ages may return, the Stone Age may return on the gleaming wings of science, and what might now shower immeasurable material blessings upon mankind, may even bring about its total destruction. Beware, I say: time may be short."

It was as if it were impossible to separate Eden from Armageddon, to summon up the one without calling up the ghost of the other. Eleven years after Churchill's Fulton speech, years that saw the nuclear secret pass into the hands of the Soviets, the development of the hydrogen bomb and the ICBM, one of the foremost shapers of foreign policy in our age was to wonder that "the survival of our civilization must be entrusted to a technology so out of scale with our experience and with our capacity to grasp its implications." You cannot beat Centipede at his own game. You cannot play on his red robe and hope to win. You cannot gamble the last thing. Like the abstractions of the War Planners, the gambling games of Centipede take on a life of their own, become their own justification. The more intense the rivalry of the opponents, the more dependent the players of the game are upon each other. One becomes one's enemy in order to outthink him, one needs one's enemy in order for the game to continue. The rivalry, stamped as an image on the language that contains it, is self-perpetuating. Its rarefied terms are a kind of utopia, beyond the realm of the human, where the abstractions of the Nuclear Age move to the seductive, unheard music of a score we are forbidden to play. Action becomes shadow. Shadow, parody. Caught in Centipede's toils, the "realists" of politics try to liberate us from the world we have created by some formula drawn from their descriptions of that world. But reality can never be abolished by its description, because that description is a part of it. Dancing at the edge of chaos, out of which human consciousness came, and into which it may return, the War Planners' strategies fly apart under the sheer weight of information they must bear and of consequences that multiply and flow over the boundaries given to any mind, to any system, to predict.

. .

In the Pentagon the encoder is sending the test message to relays in Maryland and West Virginia, then on to the satellites above the equator. In the Kremlin the decoder digests a tape that translates the message:

Interference by casual water, ground repair or a hole, cast or runway made by a burrowing animal, a reptile or a bird occurs when a ball lies in or touches any of these conditions or when the condition interferes with the player's stance. . . . A ball is "lost" if (a) it is not found or . . .

In the narrow room in the Pentagon basement the decoder taps out the answer relayed by the satellites from the other side of the earth.

So-called simple machines were developed in the cradles of civilization. . . . Not only the simple implements for lifting water (the "shadoof" in Egypt and the "chigir" in Mesopotamia) but also the so-called "sakiz."

Linked with their radar and telephone wires and microwave frequencies, the complex of locks and counterlocks, the keys that hang from the panels, the missiles are dreaming in their silos. The wires and switches and terminals that connect the system to itself are humming with their same mindless tasks. A general circles the air in a plane called *Looking Glass*, always aloft to give the command to fire. Somewhere a man follows the president with a briefcase full of codes. In a concrete room in Nebraska, deep under a mountain in Colorado, the giant screens scan the world.

At one minute to midnight all bets are off. The bluff and the posturing, the politics and the maneuvering have come to an end. The game begins to dictate its own solution.

6

By October of 1981, the MX mobile basing plan was dead. Finally, neither moral nor even strategic arguments killed the MX system, but expediency. The political price was too high. Jimmy Carter, the president who had scoffed at the MX and then had fought to build it, had won only one of the western states – Texas – in his successful election bid in 1976. In 1980, the new president, Ronald Reagan, had won them all. Reagan's ties to conservative politicians in the Great Basin were deep and some were longstanding. When the Great Basin turned against the missiles, Reagan did too. The governors of Nevada and Utah, who had at first welcomed the missiles, reversed themselves when they saw the system's social and ecological cost. For they were met with the resistance of whole sections of the Great Basin, as ranchers and environmentalists joined in opposing the system. The Western Shoshone peoples mobilized their resources to stop the obscenity of the missile on sacred lands. Only a few Indians in the basin came out in favor of the MX, at least for a time. Some of the Gosiutes thought the bases might mean jobs. Finally, the Mormon Church spoke out. In May of 1981, Church President Spencer W. Kimball issued an eloquent statement denouncing the project:

Our fathers came to this western area to establish a base from which to carry the gospel of peace to the peoples of the earth. It is ironic and a denial of the very essence of that gospel that in this same general area there would be constructed a mammoth weapons system potentially capable of destroying much of civilization.

The mobile basing system was no longer a reality. The Reagan administration had moved on to another strategy, one not tied to SALT II or any other treaties, in which the goal was not stalemate, but victory. Ratification of SALT II became a dead issue. The Soviets had reinforced their missile silos. The MX was still vulnerable. The new and desperate strategy that was being talked of in Washington was to protect the missiles by turning them over to the mechanical operations of radar systems and computers. There would be no human decision making, no debate. The missiles would be launched at the first warning of a Soviet attack. In Europe, U.S. soldiers rehearsed the mass burial of battlefield casualties in a gesture that was intended not to be lost on Soviet intelligence. Soon the even more lethal fantasy of Star Wars would replace the missile system that Reagan had renamed "Peacekeeper" in his administration's defense priorities.

Even though its mobile basing system was gone, the MX missile itself remained alive. If its rationale had changed a half-dozen times, the weapon still survived, a sort of revenant that had to be placated by new theories, new strategies. Old and discredited solutions to the missiles' vulnerability reappeared from time to time, and would not go away. In Utah, where defense firms stood to win hundred-million-dollar contracts from continuing development of the missile, there came from the Mormon Church only a strange silence. In November of 1986 the first four of the MX rockets were inserted into old silos in a remote missile field in Wyoming. They were already obsolete.

..

The Cold War is over. Arms accords once thought almost impossible are being reached between us and the inheritors of the Soviet Union, and missiles are actually being destroyed. Perhaps, as some would argue, the arms race has been vindicated, not as strategy, but as an instrument of policy. We have pauperized our enemies. Their empire no longer exists. Still the weapons that remain are many times what are necessary to obliterate the planet, and while old weapons are being destroyed by treaty, new ones, many times more dangerous, still live, if for the moment only in terms of massive research projects. It is as if, like children who know better, we are nevertheless reluctant to entirely give up our fables. Freed for the time of the nightmare of the MX, those vast tracts of the Great Basin still exist as they have largely existed since long before the beginning of history; they are still fearsomely unpeopled, waterless, harsh, and incredibly lovely, a daunting backdrop to our pretensions and our littleness.

The inhabitants of the basin, the ranchers and Indians, the government officials and the citizens of the towns and hamlets in the desert who fought and killed the MX system, did so because they saw a way of life and a place they loved in jeopardy. I like to think that the fight penetrated beneath their just fears for their own safety, their own piece of the earth, and that it touched something deep in them, something that endures.

..

So the system is gone, that dinosaur, that anachronism, relegated to the catalog of similar fictions that haunt the western landscape: Cíbola, Quivira, the River of the West, the Dream Mine . . . swindles, hoaxes, fakes. Some imagined what would be the system's legacy: a series of empty roads leading nowhere in the desert, loops turning in on themselves, a ruin of half-dug foundations and abandoned sheds with the weeds pushing up through the cracks, a monument to a civilization that had bankrupt itself. Not even this came to be. Yet somewhere the plans for the system still survive, if not as a reality, then as some racial scar, something deep in memory. Once thought, it can be thought again. The culture that tried to dream its collective and violent dream into concrete and steel and atomic matter is still intact; those same neurons and fibers and chromosomes burdened with their deadly knowledge still exist ticking off like some lethal interest in the brains of our politicians and military leaders and engineers. The pressures, the fears, the political rivalries, the intimate, unspoken things so subtle they cannot be examined, the tissues of a system of belief – they too are still there. And so the MX missile inexorably lumbering from shelter to shelter is still there. It exists in anyone who has ever thought about it. In anyone who, for even a moment, imagined it stretched out against the desert floor. And even when the last man or woman who has so much as remembered its name is dead, it will still exist. It will exist as a literature, a literature of testimonies, reports, classified documents, press releases; of transcripts, tables, half truths, fictions, lies. A literature of acronyms and neologisms, of charts and exhibits, where for human memory is substituted the microchip, for plot's sinuous unwindings the record of statistical outcomes to imaginary battles in unthinkable wars. A literature with neither passion nor love nor irony. A literature of neither laughter nor desire.

News from Nowhere

1 THE DAM

Park full of people in blue overalls and khaki shirts – low flimsy white town with greenery. . . . Barren mountains full of silver, iron, gold, aluminum, Aztec turquoise, sulphur, that looked as if they would ring if you hit them with a hammer . . . the landscape "all heaved up and then baked again" – flat basin of deep red, with whitish expanse that looked like water – gray and blue mists – blue inky clouds, as if for a storm.

By two thirty in the afternoon the temperature in the little desert railroad town of Las Vegas, Nevada, peaked. A hundred ten, a hundred twenty degrees. Edmund Wilson noted in his journal that men and women and children were milling around the only two patches of green there were, the lawns in front of the courthouse and the depot.

Victor Castle was one of the hundreds of people who slept out on those lawns at night. The morning after he got in, Castle and three friends drove out to Boulder City. They looked at the housing the Six Companies consortium was slapping together for the workers at the dam. It would be months before the town could be occupied. Then they went on to the camp called Rag City, where whole families of squatters had thrown up a huddle of tents and crude shelters of wood and cardboard and flattened tin cans. In Rag City, Las Vegas water was going for two gallons for fifteen cents, five gallons for a quarter. Most of the Rag City people dipped their supply from the gritty brown water of the hole someone had dug in the river bank.

Castle got a job working in the road gang boarding house, where four waiters served 350 sweating, half-naked men at a stretch, scarcely clearing the plates from one batch when another came along. After two days he quit. He wrote that he'd rather mooch on the main stem than work in 140-degree heat for two dollars a day and meals, and even then have $1.50 a month taken out of his pay for insurance that didn't even cover heat exhaustion. At the dam site itself it was so hot that the gas tanks on the equipment exploded by spontaneous combustion. If a man was dumb enough to try to pick up a crowbar without gloves he could end up with second-degree burns. In the two days Castle was in camp he'd seen two men brought in unconscious from the heat. One was dead before they could even drive him to the hospital in Las Vegas.

By the spring of 1932 Boulder City had been built, and the families of the dam workers poured in from the shanties of McKeeversville and Rag City. The new city was the ultimate company town, a little version of Calvin's Geneva out on the desert, run by a vice-hating puritan and one of the Six Companies thugs who had made his mark busting Wobbly heads in Las Vegas. As for the Wobblies, their drive to rebuild themselves had died in the heat and dust of the dam, killed by the Great Depression and their own brave illusions.

By December of 1934 Hoover Dam was virtually complete. It rose in the air of Black Canyon taller than the Empire State Building, the largest construction project the world had ever seen. Soon the giant generators would be in place, spinning out immense kilowattage to light Los Angeles and drive its new factories and to keep the lights burning all night long on Fremont Street in Las Vegas. Before long, the cribs of the Skidway and the road houses lining Boulder Highway would be gone and Las Vegas would become a place of increasingly rationalized sin. The two cities, the Puritan City on the road to Black Canyon, and the City of Sin, were still connected by the power lines that rose out of the dam.

There is a story that deep inside the dam's four and a half million tons of concrete lies the corpse of a worker. No such accident ever happened. But this is of little account: we know the penalty we must pay for such monstrous works. We know a worker lies buried in the dam.

And little by little the dam silts up. The water becomes sedimentary and brackish, more and more destroying the desert land it once irrigated.

Slowly, inevitably, the Colorado River eats into the foundations of the dam.

2 THE PHILOSOPHER

The Philosopher is making his way toward Las Vegas at eighty-five miles an hour. Outside the windows of the car the charred landscape wavers in the brutal light.

The Philosopher has a theory about the desert. The Philosopher has a theory about everything. In his mind, the desert is America itself. Weary of the embarrassment of culture, which hangs on him like a seedy bathrobe, the *not*-ness of the desert fascinates him. He has been reading Tocqueville. But instead of the institutions, societies, clearings in the woods, prisons, workshops, courthouses, and counting houses his countryman found in the new land, he finds the desert, leveling all values, making them all equally insignificant, and, thus, like the hummocks of brush and the outlines of the Joshua trees set against in the clear, hard light, equally original. In his mind the desert spreads outward from its center, swallowing everything. He sees it as a movie, an infinite panning shot. The Philosopher's map of America is like those nineteenth-century atlases that found at the continent's heart a Great American Desert, featureless, almost impassable, a blank space between two coasts. Driving into a kind of vortex, he surrenders himself to the imploding tunnel of his description of the land.

The desert doesn't think, therefore doesn't understand that it exists. It holds no mirror up to its strenuous beauty. Says nothing. Knows nothing. Transparent as glass, what can one make of it? It becomes another text. (One doesn't cruise this one: one zooms into it, inscribing one's description of it on its transparency.) The United States is the oldest country in the world, Gertrude Stein once said, because it has been in the twentieth century longest. It is this ancient source of the future the Philosopher longs for, this history-less, nostalgia-less place that he calls America. He himself is afflicted with nostalgia – not for the past, with its cultural gimcracks, its tarted-up toga of history, but for what he terms a nostalgia for the future.

The Philosopher speaks to no one. Not to the joggers who repel him with their manic hygiene, not the breakdancers on the corners of the streets, not to the truckers he sees briefly reflected in the rear-view mirror of his rental car as he zooms beyond them. The Philosopher does not speak, nor does he listen. He only sees. Sight: the most metaphysical of the senses. He notes the words stenciled on his rear-view mirror: *Caution: objects in this mirror may be closer than they appear.*

Where Tocqueville slogged on foot through the mud if there were no roads, took broken-down stagecoaches or grass-bellied horses if there were, chugged up and down rivers in rackety steamboats, lived in one-room pioneer cabins and Indian villages, his notebook always by him, his countryman in the Chrysler surrenders himself to the luxury of speed. And how convenient it is, after all, this machine, so good for little commando raids on the consciousness of a new land, an air-conditioned cocoon spun out of the articulations of theory. The Philosopher pushes the button and the window of his rental car slides down. The desert enters in a blast of heat and the acrid smells of sage and creosote. The Philosopher pushes the button and the window rises.

3   SIGNS

The Sign is everything here. It looms above the landscape, immense, aggressive, insistent. Even the familiar logos of gas stations and fast-food restaurants are Brobdingnagian, competing with the cries of those that front the casinos. A team of architects from the East drove down the Strip and learned that you take in the Sign before anything else. For them Fremont Street was nothing but one immense neon false-front, casinos flowing into each other behind a single popping and sizzling façade in colors so intense they paled the daylight. You consume the sign here, not that to which it points. Beyond the sign is metaphysical darkness. A world that cannot name itself, that gropes in anguish in its inky chaos. When Jean Baudrillard, who is speeding across the desert to rendezvous with this predestined place, arrives, he will find in Las Vegas the ultimate tribute to his work: a city that imitates his categories. It is a simulacrum of the simulacra of his thought. Is this not, indeed, Utopia? Where the idea becomes the pure environment, a kind of gigantic bottle that shuts out anything but itself?

4   TREADMILLS TO OBLIVION

At Caesars Palace a moving sidewalk sucks the Tourist into some strange version of Rome, if Rome, as Fellini now and then suggested, were a movie set. But what movie would this be? In the enclosed shopping mall, the Tourist finds a faux Roman street, with fountains, a café, shops selling expensive leather jackets, reproductions of artifacts from museums around the world. On the domed ceiling, the clouds pick up the tints of dawn, then blaze to noon, then slowly fade into a gentle sunset. Twilight comes, the stars wink on, the cycle starts again. The pathos of a whole day has been canned in a few minutes of sadness. Ejected by the sidewalk, back on the featureless, blazing noon of the Strip, the Tourist is at a loss, until the treadmill of the Mirage sucks him into an indoor jungle, acoustically punctuated by the clash of a million slot machines' electronic distributions of fortune. City of treadmills! Even at the airport a moving sidewalk had taken him to his rental car. From hidden speakers somewhere the voices of comedians whose names are familiar only to those who go to the shows in the casinos had told him lame jokes and warned him to keep to the right and watch his step.

The Tourist is on vacation. To be on vacation is to taste, if only faintly, what it means to be free. Free of the sinister dictatorship of the calendar, of the everlasting burden of work, free above all, of the need to choose. The disembodied voices coming over the moving sidewalks give the Tourist his instructions, prompt his needs to see, to be stimulated, to consume. And everything is possible. The ambience of the casino's interior suggests this: the banquets of cheap food, the fictive luxuries of flocked wallpaper and mirrored ceilings, the floor shows where the nakedness of women is offered impartially to everyone. The Tourist stretches himself out, luxuriates. He has placed the world permanently on hold. Here all hierarchies melt, are reconstituted under the democratic nightstick of Luck. Devalued, stripped of its moral significance, money becomes the universal solvent and the true Democracy. Standing in line at the buffet, waiting for the topless review to start, in silk shirts and tractor hats and message tee-shirts and sport coats bought in Palm Springs, we know what the Tourist knows – that we are all one.

In the corridors of the Mirage, white tigers prowl in a white boudoir, surrounded by white trees, white cliffs, white rocks, while on a television monitor their tamers discourse in Teutonic accents on the tigers' rarity. Farther on is the dolphin habitat. An odd word, "habitat," the Tourist thinks. Isn't everything here a habitat, thermostatically controlled, sealed off? Outside the desert sizzles in heat. Inside the casino hums in its dark orbit, beyond time, beyond space. It is a country in itself, with its own flag, its own constitution, its own rules. Like some huge iron lung, the air conditioners endlessly recirculate the exhausted air from the lungs of the tourists, the hum of their machinery drowned out by the pinging chatter of the machines. This place, pretending to be so foreign, isn't it oddly familiar, after all? With its piped-in music, its ostentatious displays of leisure, of food, of sexual availability, is this not a strange, mutant version of the worlds imagined by Bellamy and Fourier? This is Pleasure Industrialized. Back outside the Mirage, frequently spaced signs tell the Tourist of its main attraction:

THE VOLCANO ERUPTS DAILY EVERY 15 MINUTES AFTER DARK UNTIL
MIDNIGHT, EXCEPT IN INCLEMENT WEATHER.
THE RED FLASHING LIGHT DENOTES INCLEMENT WEATHER.

5   THE CAGE

Even in the umbilical of the jetway the Gambler had noticed the sound, faint at first, then louder, increasingly more familiar, cheerful. It was as if, walled up in some padded chamber, he could hear the blood corpuscles caroming through his arteries. Once inside the airport itself, the sound became a high, cheerful jangle and roar. This sound the Gambler heard was the ringing of the slot machines. The machines were the first altars on the sands of the new country.

Before there was money, a man might gamble a bow, a blanket, a horse, perhaps his wife. Gambling is a magical form of barter, a transaction in which the exchange is always radically unequal. But the thing one gambles becomes subtly different the moment it is staked. It enters a magic realm in which it becomes charged with the energies, risks, possibilities of the game. Yet at the same time, it becomes oddly devalued. Now it represents only an abstract token, an emptiness waiting to be filled with hope, aggression, and desire according to the unforeseen opportunities of the game. So, in order to play, the Gambler must go to the Cage. It is the Cage that makes gambling possible.

You've heard the fairy tale of the princess who could spin straw into gold? Behind the imaginary bars of the Cage sit those postsexual antiprincesses, the cashiers who spin gold into straw. At the Cage the ordinary bills passed across the counter come back as chips, spill out in nickels and quarters into the little plastic buckets emblazoned with the casino crest, cornucopias of possibility. Liberated from the vulgar economies of the everyday, from its value in terms of work, or saving, or denial, money undergoes an awful transubstantiation at the Cage: now it represents not its ghostly missing part, all that it cost in effort and care, but a magical possibility.

The Gambler moves away from the Cage, a plastic container, disturbingly reminiscent of his last visit to a delicatessen, held chalicelike between his hands. Before staking a chip, he has entered a symbolic realm.

6 GANGSTERS

The Gangsters have left only a few visible traces. The vulgarity of their hotels and casinos (for they were the first Americans who, having lost their history, were replacing it with one taken over from Hollywood, which had turned them from off-book businessmen into tragic figures) has so familiarized itself that it no longer shocks or amuses or offends. What the movies offered in a ghostly version on the screen was what Las Vegas promised in the flesh. Both Hollywood and Las Vegas were not places but floating promises of liberation from the places we had come from, from family, history, class. Thus the Gangsters who founded contemporary Las Vegas saw its site as desert in a moral sense, as a blank slate, a landscape upon which to impose their visions, and as a machine for extracting money from desire.

The only cameras allowed in casinos are those we never see. And we always know they are there. Above the false ceiling of the casino, behind peep-holes and one-way mirrors, are the closed-circuit television networks that continually watch the action. The security system is a fossilized remnant of the nervous systems of those paleo-Gangsters. Ever alert to the card-counter who might jimmy the casino's edge, the dealer who might collude with a customer, the shill who might drop a hundred-dollar chip into the front of her dress, the security system externalizes the Gangsters' own paranoia. The complex operation of the casino's inner life is analogous to those signs blazing outside it which the architects Venturi and Brown and Izenour saw – signs that "shout their gorgeous cacophony, but hide their constraining order."

So the first generation of Gangsters founded the city with money from their crimes, leavened by the pension funds of Midwestern truck drivers, and the projections – so amply justified – of a constant infusion of dollars from the tourist suckers. Utopia is a country, after all, and all countries have their tax collectors. The Gangsters were nothing more than business-men who had seized the privilege of collecting a tax on our desires for sex, for success, for action, for oblivion. How easily these rough men outgrew their origins and settled into a comfortable sort of Chamber of Commerce of Vice existence! True, a few had to be iced off, kidnapped, taken out of the game — but how very few they turned out to be. And how easily they and their surviving associates were replaced in almost seamless transitions by their heirs, the corporate managers of pleasure. It is all part of the in-creasing gangsterization of American life. The taxes on our desires are now collected by corporations who advertise on network TV.

7   LIBERACE

When the winds blow once more through the empty corridors of these false-front mausoleums, we will know that there is something Egyptian about this place. We will know it by the monuments that rise, purposeless, out of the desert; we will know it when we discover that here is where the Celebrities have come to die, embalmed inside the temples of their own personae. The museum is difficult to find because it is part of a shopping strip, and looks, in fact, not like a museum at all but like a shopping strip building. Inside are his pianos, his automobiles, the glass cases filled with his costumes, his plaques, and trophies.

Grinning from the photographs on the walls, he hangs here distributed, the *berdache* of this place, magician of the casino stages, eternally camping behind that golden grin, entombed by the monstrous costumes loaded down with sequins and metallic thread, the leaden tail-coats, the seventy-five-pound capes. Even his cars, like ceremonial hearses, are laden with mirrors, with sequins. Is it true that he had so many plastic surgeries on his face that he could not close his eyes? Sleepless before his own image he spends his long nights putting in the medicinal drops that took the place of tears.

8   DANCING ON THE FEET OF CHANCE

There is a story everyone knows about Nick the Greek, when he was old and broke and reduced to playing for small change in the card rooms of

Gardena. Someone asked him how it felt to have come from such heights to this. He turned on the questioner and said, "It's action, isn't it?"

Action is a locus, a point of charged energy, a void without a landscape, without history. It speaks of pure, liberating disconnection from anything but its own rhythms, its own surge. So you bet. You bet your lunch, you bet your pants, you bet your paycheck. You bet everything just to feel it. Moment by moment your life ticks away. But at the edge of this action you are never more alive. No one on the outside can understand it. Not your husband. Not your wife. Not your friends. Not your shrink. No one can understand the rush. Or the terror. But the moment has no duration. It has to be repeated again and again. From nothing (you are nothing here, just a person at a table) you have to create yourself. You have to create yourself again and again.

To gamble means to squeeze your life, card by card, into a story; to compress it to a point, a light blazing up at the last turn of the card that is action. Over and over again, dying and being reborn, you tell the story that is in your life but has become greater than that life, its envelope, its field.

What are the numbers the House is running against you? 0.6 percent? 5.26 percent? 20 percent? This is the true cost of gambling: this knowledge is the real price of the game. Because the game is rigged and you know it. Little by little the casino's edge eats into you. Little by little it chews you away. The ball that stutters around the frets of the roulette wheel has no memory; the Gambler is cursed with the inability to forget.

But for just this moment, this entry into the liberating territory of Luck, he must forget. That's the trick. The Gambler stares out over the green tables of the casino like Moses gazing over the Promised Land. The little tremors of anticipation race each other up and down the nerves of his legs. He is conscious only that he will win. He fingers the chips in his hand. He could laugh for joy.

9   THE PHILOSOPHER AND THE GREAT WHORE

Rising up before him in the night, all at once, "bathed in phosphorescent lights," is his true destination, "sublime Las Vegas." And yet, like some long-awaited assignation, the physical consummation seems anticlimactic. The city is too open to his categories, too shameless in its pandering to his terminology. Like some aging yet oddly inexperienced whore, who in her eagerness shows everything all at once, the town has no mystery. The Philosopher, who has invented the useful concept of hyperreality, has resurrected the notion of the simulacra, ideas whose very shadows Las Vegas pants to inhabit, finds the town, in spite of its sublimity, beneath contempt. The visit to the capital city of his vision of the future is, after all, less charming than incest, or a freeway in L.A. A few *mots* tossed off as an afterthought, like a quick feel in a hotel corridor and he is gone. He drives out of Las Vegas with the window rolled up. He doesn't see, over the rim of the horizon, the vast wedge of concrete driven into the gorge, hear the hum of the dynamos that drive the power that lights the city. The Philosopher turns the air conditioner up a notch, and once more on the asphalt arrow of highway enters the abstraction of desert.

10 LEARNING FROM LAS VEGAS

The women keep coming up to the Gambler, proffering drinks, proffering Keno, proffering change. "Hi, I'm Krystal from Boise," the nametags say. "I'm Sheri from Sacramento." "I'm Debbi from Chicago." They all have nametags and they all have smiles and the horrible thing is that the smiles are genuine. The smiles detach themselves from their bodies. They float there, above their nametags, ready to be plucked. A kiss left by the Philosopher, who is no longer there.

Later, fuzzy with liquor, needing to piss, the Gambler loses his way in Caesars, finds himself in a little rotunda surrounded by boutiques. Above him looms the familiar marble shank of the David of Michelangelo, his cloak casually draped over his shoulder, surveying with his sightless marble eyes some scene of which only marble can dream. This David, the Gambler reads, is an exact replica of the one in Florence, carved from the same mother-stone. Standing there, under the shadow of a six-pound marble testicle, all history and time are canceled in the dark zone between this figure and his original. Between these two points, the world loses its orbit, wobbles crazily. What is the need for the original if it can be so facilely reproduced? Shaved down to a few primitive needs, can the Gambler himself be reproduced?

The Gambler finds the can and makes his way back to the casino floor. Later still, he comes to another heroic statue, one he's been searching for. It is of Joe Louis, the great boxer. His pedestal is low, the statue almost accidentally placed. The boxer crouches as if in the casino itself, his fists encased in their marble gloves. Since the Gambler last saw this statue a small television monitor has been added. It is as if television must testify to the reality of everything, the tigers in their cages at the Mirage, this gladiator. Again and again on the little screen Joe Louis pounds Max Schmeling to the canvas. The Gambler remembers the saddest photograph he knows, from Mario Puzo's book on Las Vegas. The photo has no caption: none is needed. It is of Joe Louis, broke, reduced to living on tips and the charity of the casinos. He stands outside one of the hotels, his sport shirt untucked, a cigarette casually held at his side, his eyes filled with something so terrible you don't want to know it.

The Gambler is a fake, like everything here except the green bills and hard coins the casino owners take to their banks. He has stolen titles to his musings from Fred Allen and from Friedrich Nietzsche, both of them dead, and from a group of smart-aleck architects and from everyone else, knowing full well that titles, like faces, can't be copyrighted. He has stolen ideas from a half-baked French philosopher. Now he has put a few quarters in a video poker machine. On the way out of the Showboat he tells someone that he came within one card of hitting a royal flush. Some casino wise guy overhears him. "And they didn't give you nothin' for that?" the wise guy says.

The Gambler looks back on the casino, the tables with their clacking dice and fluttering cards, the nags galloping across a dozen television screens while the horse players hunch in their carrels like scholars in the reading room of some museum, the cocktail girls negotiating the crowded floor with their trays full of drinks and aprons full of change. Everywhere machines are pinging and spinning, disgorging their hard little pellets of happiness, swallowing someone's life a nickel at a time. In a forlorn little alcove the Keno players are sitting at their desks like passengers waiting for the next ferry across the Styx. He has a vision of naked men squatting in the dust. It is the beginning of culture or its end. They are gambling.

11   OUR REVELS NOW ARE ENDED . . .

Keep going. Past Fremont Street, past the garish casinos on the Strip, which by daybreak have lost their hold on the landscape. The neon signs, which imposed their blazing shouts on the darkness, now dimmed, show only the bizarre, oddly naked offers of the casino facades. Abruptly, the town ends. Only the zone of rusted beer cans that the architects who last surveyed the city found mediating between town and the vast, treeless expanse of the Mojave Desert mark this transitional space. Here the casinos "turn their ill-kept backsides toward the local highway." There is nothing else. Like the false-fronts of some old western main street, built overnight atop a lode of silver or gold that ran out its course in a year or two, you know that Las Vegas itself could, over night, blow away, the rough magic of gangsters and hoteliers disappearing like the trembling lines of heat mirage.

12 THE MEADOWS

Green grass. Willows. The little stream meandering through the valley. Thirty-two hours without water across the bleak desert from the Muddy, the oxen stumbling, about to give out. Then come the Meadows.

The water of the springs is very clear: they are from 20 to 30 feet in diameter, and at the depth of two feet the white sand bubbles all over as tho it was the bottom, but upon wading in, there is no foundation there, and it has been sounded to a depth of 60 feet, without finding bottom: and a person cannot sink to the armpits, on account of the strong upward rush of the water.

The third day was the Sabbath (honor it and keep it holy). They made a bower of willows to shield them from the brutal sun, prayed, and sang songs of Zion. That first summer they cleared the ground, planted oats, corn, peas, beans. When they looked at their well-watered plots they thought they could see the corn grow.

They made peace with the Indians, baptized them, hired them to help clear the brush and make adobes for the fort. Looked forward to the time when they could send for their women and children. But the soil turned out to be filled with alkali, and the crops died slowly all summer long. Still they kept working, preaching.

A band of miners came out, sent by the Prophet, Seer, and Revelator in Salt Lake. The miners hired the Indians to pack the lead ore down the steep trail to the improvised smelter. The Indians quit after one load. Later on, four Paiutes lugged ore alongside the mule train in exchange for pants. The Paiutes walked barefoot through the snow to save their moccasins.

Then the miners and the settlers fell out with each other. There was too much foreign matter in the lead to smelt it properly in their primitive fur-naces and they abandoned the diggings. (The foreign matter turned out to be silver. Later speculators lugged it out by the bushel basket.) A few days after the diggings were abandoned two miners came back with a cart to salvage their supplies. The Indians had already destroyed all the improve-ments. Then the colonists themselves were called home. A year after the last colonists left an itinerant missionary came through the settlement. He spoke with the Indians. Of the colonists, their life, their improvements, there was scarcely a trace. "There seems to be but very little 'Mormon' in them," he wrote. "And they showed me on their fingernails how much."

Night and day at Las Vegas Boulevard North and Washington Avenue the cars go whizzing by. Out on the desert are rising the steel-girded walls of the Emerald City. There is no longer a fort, a green meadow. No gushing spring. No little stream, cold and clear as a millrace.

13   THE PROPHET

Before the whites came to the desert, a Paiute shaman with prophetic gifts foretold that a people from across the ocean would come to take the coun-try. Every night, for one or two years, he named all the mountains and said the Indians would lose them. He was a very old man when the Mormons first came to settle on the Muddy River and the prophecy came true. And how many remember the names of the mountains anymore in Las Vegas?

There shall be sung another golden age,
    The rise of empire and of arts,
The good and great inspiring epic rage,
    The wisest heads and noblest hearts

· ·

Westward the course of empire takes its way;
    The four first acts already past,
A fifth shall close the drama with the day;
    Time's noblest offspring is the last.

George Berkeley

Coyote's Return

All along Coyote's path were signs stuck to the telephone poles and on the boarded-up windows of the stores. They were stuck to walls and the kiosks like flaking layers of skin:

CENTER FOR SOMATIC STRUCTURES

RELATIONSHIP COUNSELING FOR MEN

WING GLIDING

HERBOLOGY

BI-SEXUAL WOMEN'S PARTY

Coyote looked at the signs, thinking maybe the People had left them for him. He cocked his head. But he didn't know who had left this strange writing behind. Or if they were People at all. He trotted on. His feet hurt in the new boots he'd won playing handgame with the Paiutes over in Bishop on the Fourth of July.

Everywhere on the street Coyote saw people with their goods fill-

ing grocery carts, heaped up in ragged bundles. They were mostly sitting and smoking, hands extended, pitiful. Many had strange hair, roached up like the Utes, or twisted in cunning loops like Black Man or in long queues like the *tsanimmani*. This encouraged Coyote. He felt friendly toward them.

He saw some figures sitting against a building, and they were dressed in rags and leather. They had a dog with them who was wearing a bandana around his neck. He thought they might be People. But when he got close enough to get a whiff he smelled only Ghost underneath the sweat and rags. The dog pattered after Coyote but Coyote curled his lips over his teeth and the dog scuttled away. So, he thought, there were Ghost dogs too. They only impersonated dogs. You had to take care. Coyote trotted off, overcoming a powerful desire to lift his leg on the corner of Cody's Books.

Coyote was no longer a god. He was just an old Indian in patched overalls, playing tricks on Black Man, cheating Mexican at horse races. Elder Brother Wolf was gone and Coyote's children were scattered all over the earth. After all those years he wanted some company. He wanted to find his children, the People, to see what had become of them. For a while he hadn't known where to go. He consulted his tail. The tip of his tail had nothing to tell him. He consulted the fur in the fat part of his tail. The fur in the fat part of his tail was out to lunch. He consulted his asshole. His asshole gave good advice. Go to Berkeley, his asshole said. There are trees and shelter there. There are creeks that flow into the great Western Sea. There must be People in Berkeley.

"Get on across the street! Get on across the street!"

Beyond the thin ribbon of Bancroft Avenue there was laughter from the street people and loungers on the steps of the Student Union. A shaman was striding up and down in patched-up goggles and a scraggly beard.

"Do you know the functional definition of genocide?" the shaman said. "Two Republicans screwing each other. The difference between Republicans and Democrats is that Republicans screw but don't come. The Democrats come but don't screw . . ."

"And I called to him, and I preached the word, and I said, 'Do you know what Love is?' and he said, 'Yes, I know what Love is. I have just come out of one transvestite bar and I am going into another one.'"

Across from the shaman in glasses was another shaman in a K Mart necktie and Hawaiian shirt, with red hair that flamed like a fire above his skull. The two shamans stood face to face, barking at each other, testing their powers.

The light changed and Coyote pushed across the asphalt, elbowed by the crowds of people, students, skateboarders, tourists. Surely one of these wizards would know where he could find his children.

Coyote trotted toward the shamans, his tongue out, panting eagerly. But the Red Haired Shaman and the Shaman in Goggles couldn't see Coyote. They were shouting so loudly at each other that Coyote just flittered between them like the shadow of a little bird. He trotted away.

"The greatest, the most stupendous event in the history of the world. A man, a man resurrected from the dead!" the Red Haired Shaman was saying.

"It happens all the time," said the Shaman in Goggles. Laughter spilled over the rest of the words. All Coyote could hear was the men's ranting and the students' laughter. These men couldn't tell Coyote where his children had gone.

The students poured out of the buildings, flowed protozoa-like among the concrete urns and bogus Corinthian columns. They just flowed by, their ears plugged with earphones, jigging to an unheard music, idiot grins on their faces, books under their arms. Under their tee-shirts and sparse beards they looked like two-car garages in the suburbs. Coyote's nose twitched. Coyote wanted to grab them, to shake them in his paws, yell at them. Make an asshole out of himself. Where are you going? he wanted to shout. Where are you going? We have to find the People! But the students didn't stop – only a few paused and then they too drifted off.

Out on the plaza a pay phone rang. Coyote knew it was for him. He picked it up. Into his ear came a long, low moan. A moan that seemed to be coming from the other side of the earth. A moan that was like a chuckle, too. Coyote's asshole puckered with fear.

"Wolf?" he said. "Elder Brother?"

There was no answer, only that long, low moan that was also a chuckle.

"Where are you? Are you coming around here?"

Nothing.

"I'll fix everything up for you just the way it was," Coyote cried. "I'll round up all those animals and put them back in that pen. I'll put those teeth back in those women's twats."

Nothing.

"No! Wait! I'll run Death off. It'll be just like the old days. . . ."

There was only that long, low moaning on the line.

"Where are you?" Coyote said. "Give me a hint?"

But Wolf was silent. Now there was only the distant sound of wind. The sound of wind coming from a thousand miles away.

"Well, go screw yourself then!" Coyote cried. "I'll find the People without you. I'll make the world all over. . . ." But there was no sound, and he hung up the phone.

Coyote came to a place guarded by some great statues of gods or demons. His flea directed him there. His flea thought something in that place might be calling Coyote. The statues looked like something People might have made. Coyote circled three times, sniffed, lifted his leg, and went through the doors.

Inside the museum, Coyote wandered up and down, peering into the cases. Displayed in the cases were things that looked familiar, the work of People's hands. But everything was different, embalmed behind the glass. Cunning savages! Here were carved Peruvian gourds introduced by the Peace Corps, Trobriand napkin rings, "picturesque" Yoruba wood carvings of polo players with wristwatches, magistrates in curly wigs, what might be a god riding a bicycle. Totem figures from New Guinea spray-shellacked to fit the aesthetic of a Southern California surfer bar. Coyote sniffed and cocked his head. Underneath the smells of spar varnish, super-glue, model airplane cement, aniline dye there was only a faint smell of People after all. *Pah!* His mouth puckered, his lips curled back from his teeth. What it smelled like in the museum was Ghosts.

The most important material items in native Yir Yirout culture (N. Australia) were stone axes. They were a monopoly of the old men of the group who obtained them through a series of trading partners and controlled their use according to complex rules of sex, age, kinship. . . . Steel hatchets were distributed profusely and indiscriminately by Western missionaries to Yir Yirout young people and women. The effect was disruption of the traditional mechanisms of the exchange of valuables, the destruction of the social power of the old men and a revolutionary confusion of age, sex and kinship roles.

Coyote peered into a glass case, looking at all that remained of the Yir Yirout: a few murky photographs, a few strips of bark and twisted grass, an immense, ludicrously clumsy stone axe.

The present and the future, which were conceived of as simply stable continuations of the mythical past of the totemic ancestors became conceptually unstructured and uncertain and individual demoralization and cultural disintegration followed. There was a total disruption of the aboriginal social structure.

Poor Yir Yirout.

150

Outside dusk was coming. Still Coyote moved from case to case, hoping to see something familiar, to hear some object, some stone or piece of clay sing the magic song inside it. But the pieces behind the glass were silent. Their tongues had been cut out, their souls were dead. There were only the faint, dry buzz of the lights and the pale shadow of his own face reflected in the glass.

In the lobby of the museum Coyote stopped to look around. From a rack of postcards Ishi, the last wild Indian of California, stared at him. In the photograph Ishi was dressed in a coat and necktie. His hair was cut and parted according to the tradition of his tribe. They stood there, staring at each other, Coyote, the first Person, and Ishi, perhaps one of the last. The face of the man in the photograph was without pity or scorn. He was looking beyond Coyote to the land of Ghosts, but Coyote could not hear what he said or know what he felt.

It was cold. The place was empty. It smelled of emptiness. Coyote shivered and went out.

At the corner of Bancroft and Telegraph avenues the street bazaar was closing up, the sellers of tie-dyed tee-shirts and carved hash pipes and cheap jewelry were rolling up their mats in the darkening light, concessionaires were shuttering their little gypsy-wagon stands, hitching them to the cars that would tow them away. Students and street people were beginning to pour across the narrow band of asphalt that separated the world from the campus, they came and went as they pleased. The Hare Krishna chanters with their shaven heads and sherbet-pink long underwear marched by, banging drums and gongs, singing. From out of the crowd someone approached Coyote, a slovenly, haunted man with stony eyes and wild hair. He reached his hand out to Coyote and Coyote flinched back, terrified of the touch of this wild man. Then the man slipped into the crowd of gray people going away. Coyote looked down at his hand and the hairs on the back of his neck hackled. His pecker stiffened with fear. In his hand was a card.

Walt Whitman, the poet, has moved

The moon was rising, a pale, white disk above the Campanile. A satellite darted across the sky. Coyote sat on a curb and pulled off his boots and looked at his naked feet. They were covered with hair. It was getting harder and harder to make the transformation complete. Coyote thought he'd find the Red Haired Shaman or the Shaman in Goggles again, give them another try, but when Coyote looked around he saw that they had gone. And then Coyote noticed that the whole square was filled with shamans just like them. Two wizards in polka dots stood juggling clubs and pieces of fruit. Another shaman with the chalk-white face of a ghost stood on one foot as if made out of stone. A thaumaturge wandered around in greasy clothes and long hair talking to himself. There was a *berdache* in a long beard and a ragged dress. A blind man coaxed voices out of a machine. But there were no miracles here, no thunder or streaks of lightning in the evening clouds. The ghost-man saw no visions, the voices the boom-box wizard conjured were angry and confused. The *berdache* had no wisdom. The thaumaturge acted drunk or insane. It was a land of magicians with no powers, shamans with no understanding, wizards who brought back no dead, only Ghosts into a Ghost world. A copy of the *Swingers Exchange* blew against Coyote's leg and stayed there, flapping like a damaged pigeon. From the Personals flew up a narrow wail of pain . . . HAD ANY LATELY? DON'T BEAT YOUR MEAT. CALL BIANCA, 510 . . .

All at once Coyote felt ineffably alone, abandoned, lost. Lost as that long ago time when he'd opened Water Girl's jug too soon and his children had scattered in four directions across the desert. Empty as that jug when he sat there rattling it to see if even one of his children remained. Coyote's insides were rumbling. His guts were full of worms. All at once Coyote felt an overwhelming need to defecate.

A cloud moved across the sky. The moon went out. Coyote knelt on the asphalt pavement and opened his hands palms up in supplication. Then he threw back his head and howled: "whoooooooooooooo-oooooooooooooo yip yip yip yip."

But no one answered. No man, or animal, or demigod. He looked down in his palm and saw a greasy dime someone had left behind.

Coyote felt weak and cold. He scratched his left side and felt the ribs sticking out. He looked at the trash piled up in the plaza. *Pah.* He couldn't eat that stuff. His flea was almost dead from hunger too. Up in the sky, above the dark hump of hills, his daughters the Pleiades were laughing at him. Coyote scratched his balls under his overalls. It was time to go. He pulled on his boots over his paws. Clear out of here, he said to himself. Get going.

· ·

Earth gets old. The ghost-darkness spreads over the dying land. The Ghosts spread over more and more of it, gibbering and sighing in their backward way. Deep in the cellar of the museum, the bones of Coyote's children are lying in long, flat drawers. In the darkness they moan and sigh, but there is no one to bring them back. The bones clatter as if shivering with cold, clatter and fall back. In the room there is only a dead, faint smell. Buried somewhere, deep in the heart of some mountain or underground, Wolf has retreated where he hopes never to be found. His hunger is beyond remedy. His dreams are beyond desire. He is a blip on a radar screen. A sonar echo. A streak of light moving across a monitor. An impulse buried in a chip embedded in the nose cone of a missile. You cannot kill Wolf. He has purged the world of Death and become pure diagram.

Back in the darkened plaza, among the blowing paper cups, the cigarette butts, the frozen yogurt containers, the flapping newspapers, the turd Coyote left on the asphalt is crying in the dark

Coyote, Coyote, Coyote
No People Here No People

Shoshone Myths
and Their Retelling

In one of his manuscripts on the Numic peoples, John Wesley Powell gives an account of how Great Basin tales were originally told which is worth quoting:

At night by the campfire the chief of the council or some venerable man will tell one of these stories, and the elderly men of the band will enjoin especially upon the younger members to take heed of what is said. The chief relates the narrative and, whenever the circumstances are favorable, illustrates by acting a part, imitating the voice or actions of the several animal personages who are supposed to have taken part in the original scene, growling for the bear, chattering for the magpie, scolding for the Canada jay, chirping for the squirrel and hissing for the snake.

Often there is much dialogue when the elders take a part, and they will also assist in the acting. Sometimes a song is introduced in which, perhaps, the whole party will join. Perhaps while the principal actors are doing their parts, some person will interrupt them to comment on the wisdom or folly of such acts or to make some pertinent explanation for the benefit of the younger members of the tribe, and all seem much interested and greatly amused, bursting forth into loud laughter or screaming with wild delight.

So the story is in some sense a dialogue, a way of interpretation as well as a tale. The term for telling stories, both public or private, in the Shoshone and Northern Paiute tongues is literally translated as "telling each other stories." Without a ritual system in which to embed some canonical telling – the Shoshonean world was remarkably free of ritual – and with a loosely structured tribal system that was replicated in their relationship to supernatural power, individual men and women freely developed their own notions of the bonds between humanity and nature, the world and the supernatural. Thus the tales, in which so much of these relationships was set forth, always remained in some respect speculative. This generous mental environment had room, too, for more than one version of the tale, more than one explanation of the customs and features of the world we now inhabit.

We in literate societies live in cultures founded on authoritative texts, and indeed, the great religions of the Mediterranean basin are products of such works, unique, unarguable, bearing in them the voice of the divinity. Our laws, our sciences, our social orders base themselves on secular texts, whose exegesis employs armies of experts, and even in our literary occupations much scholarly effort is expended to establish the definitive text of this play or that novel. Thus it is sometimes difficult for us to imagine a world in which there was no single text of a tale, no canonical version hardened by custom and usage. For the Shoshonean people, sitting around the fire at night, the text was a series of tellings of the tales beginning long before the present one, and extending into a future that would be there as long as there were people to tell the tales and to hear them. In fact, it is more accurate to term the telling of the tale a performance, for it was nothing more than a version of something that existed in the people's collective experience, a telling in song and gesture and interaction with the audience who listened, questioned, sometimes quarreled. So, for the audience, the performances past, present, even those to come, overlapped, and the tale was memory and experience at once, local and universal at the same time.

My method of stitching together details from the whole corpus of Shoshonean myth to some extent reproduces, or tries to reproduce, a part of that experience, for by selecting details from many texts I've tried to flesh out, to re-create, a story that illuminates what I think are the essential motifs and ideas in the tales. A given telling of a Shoshonean tale may not mention the vaginal teeth of Coyote's hostesses in the Creation of People story; it doesn't need to, since we know from other tales that they are there.

On any given night a tale teller might give a longer or shorter – or even a fundamentally different version – of the tale. I might, of course, have proceeded to develop my thoughts on the ideas embedded in the tales by cross-comparison of their many versions and produced a text speckled with footnotes and cross-references that would be tedious to write and more tedious to read. I chose what I hope is at least a more readable method.

In the Southern Ute version of the Theft of Fire in Robert Lowie's collection of Shoshonean tales, first Magpie, then Hummingbird, ascend into the sky to see the direction from which fire comes, and return without success. Finally a bird called Yu'suwiv, which is unidentified, succeeds. In a Gosiute version of the Theft of Fire collected by Anne M. Smith it is either Snow-bird or Hummingbird who succeeds in spotting the fire. In Lowie's Shiv-wits version, Eagle, Chickenhawk and Woodpecker all fail and *Fish* succeeds. Are these differences meaningful? Certainly. Anthropologists such as Lévi-Strauss have made brilliant use of them. My ambition has been different. It has been to create a story that imparts its own pleasures – those pleasures in the telling and pleasures in the hearing that are, in my view, part and parcel of the deepest structures of these wonderful stories.

To be *inside* a culture is like being inside the smooth, hollow belly of Coyote's water jug. It is to be enclosed, and one understands from the inside, tacitly, intuitively, unconsciously. Any other understanding is an artifact, something made up, a fiction, an abstraction, a tool. So, after all, like everyone else, I've made up a story less about the Dust People than about myself. The Indian tales recounted in this book came out of a world that was once whole, but by the time of even the earliest attempts to record them, that world was already in fragments. And so I haven't hesitated to combine elements from various sources. And I haven't hesitated to embellish, here and there, the tales with my own small additions, as the first tellers had done. In short, I've tried to create my own approximation of the Shoshonean storytellers' art, in writing tales that are instruments for speculation and pleasure, and tributes to the wonders of their orginals, with their shrewd, deadpan humor, their monstrous slapstick and erotic joy, their magic songs and improvisations and their haunting moments of beauty.

There are some who see the old stories as sacred, the particular possession of the people out of whose lives they came and in whose languages they were first told. It is a position I respect but do not share. The one I hold sees the world's stories as possessions of all humanity. And surely seldom before have we so badly needed the Shoshonean storytellers' wisdom.

The principal collections of Shoshonean tales I've consulted are listed below:

Isabel T. Kelly, "Northern Paiute Tales," *Journal of American Folk-Lore* 51 (October–December 1938): 363–438.

Robert H. Lowie, "Shoshonean Tales," *Journal of American Folk-Lore* 37 (January–June 1924): 1–242.

Edward Sapir, "Texts of the Kaibab Paiutes and Uintah Utes," *Proceedings of the American Academy of Arts and Sciences* 65 (September 1930): 297–535.

Anne M. Smith, assisted by Alden Hayes, *Shoshone Tales* (Salt Lake City, 1993).

Julian H. Steward, "Some Western Shoshoni Myths," *Anthropological Papers, no. 31, Smithsonian Institution,* Bureau of American Ethnology Bulletin 136 (Washington DC, 1943), pp. 249–99.

Julian H. Steward, "Myths of the Owens Valley Paiute," *University of California Publications in American Archaeology and Ethnology* 34, no. 5, (Berkeley CA, 1936): 355–440.

I have also made use of the oral histories in the American Indian History Project Supported by Miss Doris Duke in the collection of the Western History Center of the University of Utah, Salt Lake City.

CHAPTER ONE: DUST PEOPLE

2 "truthful?" John C. Van Dyke, *The Desert* (1901; Salt Lake City, 1980), p.109.

11 frightened sheep. Washington Irving, *The Adventures of Captain Bonneville, U.S.A. in the Rocky Mountains and the Far West* (London, 1850), pp.212–14.

11 sold as slaves. Thomas J. Farnham, 1843, quoted in Julian H. Steward, *Basin-Plateau Aboriginal Sociopolitical Groups,* Bureau of American Ethnology Bulletin 120 (1938; Salt Lake City, 1970), p.9.

11 Paiute remembered. Margaret M. Wheat, *Survival Arts of the Primitive Paiutes* (Reno, 1967), p.17.

12 Dust People. *Handbook of North American Indians,* vol. 11, *Great Basin,* ed. Warren L. D'Azevedo (Washington DC, 1986), p.281.

13 roots, greens. For descriptions of Great Basin Indian subsistence economy, see *Handbook of North American Indians,* vol. 11; Wheat, *Survival Arts of the Primitive Paiutes;* and Steward, *Basin-Plateau Aboriginal Sociopolitical Groups.* For Shoshonean concepts of property, see Stephen C. Cappannari, "The Concept of Property Among Shoshoneans," in *Essays in the Science of Culture in Honor of Leslie A. White,* ed. Gertrude E. Dole and Robert L. Carneiro (New York, 1960). On the Gosiutes, see Carling Malouf, "The Gosiute Indians," in *Shoshone Indians, American Indian*

Ethnohistory: California and Basin-Plateau Indians (New York, 1974); Julian H. Steward, *Culture Element Distributions XXIII: Northern and Gosiute Shoshoni,* Anthropological Records, vol. 8, no. 3 (Berkeley and Los Angeles, 1943); and Floyd A. O'Neil, "The Utes, Southern Paiutes, and Gosiutes," in *The Peoples of Utah,* ed. Helen Z. Papanikolas (Salt Lake City, 1976). See also Ralph V. Chamberlin, "The Ethno-botany of the Gosiute Indians," *Proceedings of the Academy of Natural Sciences of Philadelphia, February, 1911* (April 1911): 24–41.

13 the seeds grow. *Handbook of North American Indians,* 11:634, 646, 649.

13 "for food." James H. Simpson, *Report of Explorations across the Great Basin in 1859* (1876; Reno, 1983), pp. 52–53.

14 "secretive set." Simpson, *Report,* pp. 53–54.

14 south of the Great Salt Lake. These are now made up of the Stansbury, Onaqui, and Sheeprock mountains.

14 redeem the rest of the globe. Arnold Guyot, *The Earth and Man: Lectures on Comparative Physical Geography, in Its Relation to the History of Mankind* (Boston, 1855), p. 238. Guyot first gave the lectures on which his book was based in French, in Boston in 1849.

15 "Christian heart." Guyot, *The Earth,* pp. 253–54.

15 "our griefs." Guyot, *The Earth,* p. 216.

15 to the world? Guyot, *The Earth,* pp. 97–98.

15 the Indians' food. Simpson, *Report,* p. 56.

15 "to America." Guyot, *The Earth,* p. 321.

16 the wilderness. Guyot, *The Earth,* pp. 231–32.

17 "a hog would decline." The descriptions of the trip across the desert and of the Gosiutes are from Mark Twain, *Roughing It* (Hartford CT, 1872), chap. 19.

18 dirty jokes. As I've noted, my conception of Mark Twain as Bad Boy owes a good deal to Dwight Macdonald's chapter on Twain in *Against the American Grain* (New York, 1962).

18 "afraid of anything." "Huck Finn and Tom Sawyer among the Indians," in *Mark Twain's Hannibal, Huck and Tom,* ed. Walter Blair (Berkeley and Los Angeles, 1969), pp. 94–95.

19 "doted on her." "Huck Finn and Tom Sawyer among the Indians," p. 99.

19 written at all. See Wayne R. Kime, "Huck among the Indians: Mark Twain and Richard Irving Dodge's *The Plains of the Great West and Their Inhabitants,*" *Western American Literature* 24 (February 1990): 329–30.

20 "in hell." Mark Twain to William Dean Howells, 22 September 1889. *Mark Twain–Howells Letters: The Correspondence of Samuel L. Clemens and Wil-*

liam D. Howells, 1872–1910, 2 vols., ed. Henry Nash Smith and William M. Gibson, with Frederick Anderson (Cambridge MA, 1960), 2:613.

20 "and pis-ants." Garland Hunt in 1855, quoted in Brigham D. Madsen, *Glory Hunter: A Biography of Patrick Edward Connor* (Salt Lake City, 1990), p.60.

20 camp of Gosiutes. Charles E. Dibble, "The Mormon Mission to the Shoshoni Indians, part 1," *Utah Humanities Review* 1 (January 1947): 65.

21 objection made. Malouf, "The Gosiute Indians," pp.120–22.

21 punish the Indians. Elijah Nicholas Wilson, *Among the Shoshones* (1910; Medford OR, 1971), pp.170–72.

21 Antelope Valley Indians. Steward, *Basin-Plateau Aboriginal Sociopolitical Groups*, pp.128–29. Steward says the occupants of Antelope Valley are called Gosiute by some informants, Shoshone by others. "As they cooperated and intermarried with the neighboring Deep Creek Gosiute, whose language and culture differs in no way from Shoshoni, it makes no difference what they are called" (p.128). The Gosiute are now considered a branch of the Western Shoshone. Steward gives "Antelope Jack's" village as Toiva, a spring at the northern end of Antelope Valley of three or four families.

21 were killed. James Sharp's account in the *Salt Lake Tribune*, 22 May 1960.

22 even the dogs. Wilson, *Among the Shoshones*, pp.182–85.

22 the story begins. The Indian version of these events is found in Wick R. Miller, *Newe Natekwinappeh: Shoshoni Stories and Dictionary*, University of Utah Anthropological Papers 94 (Salt Lake City, 1972), pp.86–91. This work is the source for the following quotations.

23 Dugway Mountain. Salt Lake *Tribune*, 22 May 1960. This is the source for Jim Sharp's account of the Gosiute's revenge on the mail riders.

24 a magic. For Gosiute conceptions of power see Malouf, "The Gosiute Indians," pp.81–82, and Julian H. Steward, *Culture Element Distributions: 23: Northern and Gosiute Shoshoni*, University of California Anthropological Records, vol. 8, no. 3 (Berkeley and Los Angeles, 1943), p.232.

25 rat's tail fell off. Maude Moon's story is found in Miller, *Newe Natekwinappeh*, pp.86–91.

25 Government Springs. Madsen, *Glory Hunter*, pp.86, 94.

25 next two decades. Albert B. Reagan, "The Gosiute (Goshute), or Shoshoni-Goship Indians of the Deep Creek Region, in Western Utah," *Proceedings of the Utah Academy of Sciences, Arts and Letters* 11 (1934): 46–48. See also James B. Allen and Ted J. Warner, "The Gosiute Indians in Pioneer Utah," *Utah Historical Quarterly* 39 (1971): 168. The treaty was signed by Utah Territorial Governor James Doty and Brigadier General P. E. Connor for the whites. Connor had

replaced General Albert Sidney Johnston in Utah and continued his war against the Shoshoneans. Johnston had died the year before, commanding Confederate troops at Shiloh. The treaty with the Gosiutes, like the Ruby Valley treaty that preceded it, had more to do with assuring the safe shipment of western gold and silver to finance the Union cause than with justice for the Indians.

27 "beasts of prey." 2 Nephi 5:24.

27 will bring restoration. 2 Nephi 5:22.

27 "delightsome people." 2 Nephi 30:6. The first edition of the Book of Mormon has the phrase "pure and delightsome." Current editions have returned to that original phrasing. However, see 3 Nephi 2:14–16, for an instance where converted Lamanites experienced a transformation, and "their skin became white like unto the Nephites."

28 message was clear. James A. Little, *Jacob Hamblin: A Narrative of His Personal Experience, as a Frontiersman, Missionary to the Indians, and Explorer* (Salt Lake City, 1881), pp.26–30.

28 taller than the other. John Nicholson, "The Lamanites," *Juvenile Instructor 9*, nos. 23, 25, 34 (Salt Lake City, 1874): 279–81, 303.

28 lost Israelite tribes. See the Book of Mormon, 3 Nephi 28:1–18.

28 against evil. For Indian ideas in relation to baptism see Malouf, "The Gosiute Indians," pp.148–49.

28 white clay. For the powers held to be in white clay by Shoshoneans see HDR Sciences (Santa Barbara), "Environmental Characteristics of Alternative Designated Deployment Areas: Native Americans (Nevada/Utah)," *U.S. Air Force Ballistic Missile Office*, MX *Environmental Technical Report* 21 (Norton Air Force Base CA, 1980), p.74.

28 "to become white." Miller, *Newe Natekwinappeh*, p.71.

29 once more, were fooled. Miller, *Newe Natekwinappeh*, pp.68–71.

29 "mere banditti." Richard F. Burton, *The City of the Saints and Across the Rocky Mountains to California*, ed. Fawn M. Brodie (1861; New York, 1963), p.533.

29 "forgotten people." Allen and Warner, "The Gosiute Indians in Pioneer Utah," p.176.

30 grew underground. Malouf, "The Gosiute Indians," pp.153–54.

30 want to use it. Howard R. Egan, *Pioneering the West, 1846–1878: Major Howard Egan's Diary* (Richfield UT, 1917), pp.222–23.

30 about the dream. The account of the Ghost Dance is drawn from James Mooney's classic *The Ghost-Dance Religion and the Sioux Outbreak of 1890*, ed. and abridged Anthony F. C. Wallace (1892–93; Chicago, 1965). Mooney claims (p.49) that the Ghost Dance was taken up by the Bannock, Shoshone,

Ute, and Gosiute in 1889. See also *Handbook of North American Indians*, 11:662, for an abbreviated account of the dance that distinguishes between the Nevada Paiute Wovoka's originally pacifistic vision and the more radical one promulgated by the Bannock.

30 much after that. Malouf, "The Gosiute Indians," pp.156–57, and Edna Hope Gregory, "Iosepa, Kanaka Ranch," *Utah Humanities Review* 2 (January 1948): 3–9.

31 for the cabins. Joseph H. Peck, "How I Put Down the Redskins," *Saturday Evening Post*, 23 October 1948. Joseph H. Peck, *What Next, Doctor Peck?* (Englewood Cliffs NJ, 1959), p.160.

31 seeking water for his people. Reagan, "The Gosiute (Goshute), or Shoshoni-Goship Indians of the Deep Creek Region, in Western Utah," pp.48–50.

31 detested Frank. Richard N. Ellis, "Indians at Ibapah in Revolt," *Nevada Historical Quarterly* 19 (fall 1976): 163–70. Peck, *What Next, Doctor Peck?* pp.157–58.

31 Anees Tommy. He is so referred to in the *Handbook of North American Indians*, vol. 11; other sources refer to him as "Annies Tommy" or even "Annie's Tommy."

32 Ghost Dance prophet. David L. Wood, "Gosiute-Shoshone Draft Resistance, 1917–18," *Utah Historical Quarterly* 49 (spring 1981): 179. Jack Wilson was also known by his Paiute name Wovoka.

32 needed to register for the draft. Wood, "Gosiute-Shoshone Draft Resistance, 1917–18," pp.174–75, 185–86.

32 "control situation." Ellis, "Indians at Ibapah in Revolt," p.164.

34 "or Indian agents." Peck, *What Next, Doctor Peck?* pp.190–91.

34 we won't do it. Ellis, "Indians at Ibapah in Revolt," p.166.

35 trunks and legs. The photo from the Salt Lake *Tribune*, 22 February 1918, is reproduced in Wood, "Gosiute-Shoshone Draft Resistance," p.173. For another photograph of Anees Tommy in 1940, the year of his death, see *Handbook of North American Indians* 11:265. A photograph of Antelope Jake as an old man appears in the 1919 edition of Elijah Nicholas Wilson's *Among the Shoshones*, retitled *The White Indian Boy: The Story of Uncle Nick among the Shoshones*, ed. Howard R. Driggs (New York, 1919), p.171.

35 the way he had. The account of the arrests is taken from Ellis, "Indians at Ibapah in Revolt"; Wood, "Gosiute-Shoshone Draft Resistance"; and Peck, "How I Put Down the Redskins" and *What Next, Doctor Peck?*

35 "his own purposes." Clifford Geertz, *The Interpretation of Cultures: Selected Essays by Clifford Geertz* (New York, 1973), p.347.

37 a simple one. For accounts of the handgame and its distribution see Stewart Cu-
lin, *Games of the North American Indians* (1906; New York, 1975), pp.267–
327. Jaime de Angulo gives a lively account of a game played between Paiutes
and Achumawi in his little masterpiece *Indians in Overalls* (1950; San Francisco, 1990), pp.34–39.

37 a little death. The Shoshonean myths of the handgame with the fire people are interesting to compare to Two Leggings's account of the game among the Crows, as related in Peter Nabokov, *Two Leggings: The Making of a Crow Warrior* (1967; New
York, 1970), p.26: "We are fond of gambling and the two boys taught us this. The
two Without Fires clans like to gamble against each other and their stakes are lives
of the Indians they have adopted through the medicine dreams. When a clan mem-
ber loses, his adopted child is 'eaten' by the winning clan." The Without Fires clans
are denizens of the Other Side Camp, or land of the dead in Crow mythology. Thus
to be "eaten" means to be absorbed into the winning clan in death. For people who
had so little sense of personal ownership as the Shoshones, gambling must have
been a psychologically powerful exchange.

Lévi-Strauss notes that all North American mythology affirms that to win a
game is symbolically to "kill" one's opponent. In this analysis Coyote's people
are playing a serious game indeed with the fire people in the Shoshonean tales,
and the theft of fire is a sort of extralegal solution to the stand-off between living
and dead while the game between them hangs in the balance. Consciousness is
thus a real theft, for it leads to a permanent asymmetry between living and dead,
the kind of asymmetry that Lévi-Strauss says ritual (and Shoshonean culture has
comparatively little ritual to begin with) is always trying to redress. See Claude
Lévi-Strauss, *The Savage Mind* (1962; Chicago, 1966), pp.30–33.

37 the story itself. By transforming aggression into the symbolic gestures of the
game, gambling becomes one of the arts of civilization. It is thus the perfect medium of communication between Coyote and the hostile fire people. Alan
Dundes notes the structural similarity between games and tales and applies such
an analysis to the handgame. See *The Morphology of North American Indian
Folktales* (Helsinki, 1964).

41 on their lands. See *Handbook of North American Indians* 11:592. The Salt Lake
Tribune, 14 August 1980, quotes one of the Gosiutes' attorneys as claiming that
many of the tribe's people saw the MX as a way of obtaining work, better roads,
housing and schools and that the tribe had adopted a resolution to that effect.
Still, said the attorney, they worried about their sovereignty, about water, about
timing.

42 government grant. The Salt Lake *Tribune,* 30 January 1993.

43 "and knowledge." Dante Alighieri, *Inferno,* trans. Mark Musa (Bloomington, Ind., 1971), Canto XXVI, lines 112–20.

44 "endless heights." *Inferno,* Canto XXVI, lines 130–35.

44 woman's nipple. Christopher Columbus, "Letter to the Sovereigns," quoted in Tzvetan Todorov, *The Conquest of America,* trans. Richard Howard (1982; New York, 1984), p.16.

44 Greek pun, Lewis Mumford, "Utopia, the City and the Machine," *Utopias and Utopian Thought,* ed. Frank E. Manuel (Boston, 1966), p.8.

45 "a little flat." Michel de Montaigne, *The Complete Essays of Montaigne,* trans. Donald Frame (Stanford CA, 1958), p.154. An interesting exchange: the Christian Frenchman trades the sacramental wafer, flesh of a sacrificed man, for the benign vegetable bread of the alleged cannibals. Symbolic difference is reduced to a new taste: henceforth, by sharing something (taste) irreducible to symbol, Montaigne *knows* the Brazilians.

45 "that he imagined." Montaigne, *The Complete Essays of Montaigne,* p.153.

45 Gonzalo, *The Tempest,* 2.1.139–64.

46 to Florida. Álvar Núñez Cabeza de Vaca, *La Relación,* 1542, edited and translated by Cyclone Covey as *Cabeza de Vaca's Adventures in the Unknown Interior of America* (1961; Albuquerque, 1992).

46 "my commodities." *Cabeza de Vaca's Adventures,* p.67.

47 proto-merchants. Proto-merchants because the exchanges of goods were not for profit, but part of Indian rituals of guest and host. See Rolena Adorno, "The Negotiation of Fear in Cabeza de Vaca's *Naufragios,*" *Representations* 33 (Winter 1991): 169–70, for Cabeza de Vaca's role as mediator between tribes. I have profited by her description of Cabeza de Vaca's shamanic role as well.

47 "(from Heaven.)" *Cabeza de Vaca's Adventures,* p.120.

47 would a snake. *Cabeza de Vaca's Adventures,* p.92.

47 "and we theirs." *Cabeza de Vaca's Adventures,* p.120.

47 January of 1536, The travelers thought that it was shortly after Christmas: like other things these benighted men had brought with them from Europe, time, as measured by the Christian calendar, had begun to become unhinged.

48 adventures and trials. The account of Cabeza de Vaca's return to Spain is found in the *True Relation of the Hardships Suffered by Governor Fernando de Soto and Certain Portuguese Gentlemen During the Discovery of the Province of Florida. Now Newly Set Forth by a Gentleman of Elvas,* 2 vols., trans. and ed. James Alexander Robertson, vol. 2, translation and annotations, Publication of

the Florida State Historical Society, no. 11, vol. 2 (De Land FL 1933), pp.8–13. For his adventures on the Rio de la Plata see Morris Bishop, *The Odyssey of Cabeza de Vaca* (New York, 1933). The double story told by Cabeza de Vaca is suggested by Adorno, "The Negotiation of Fear," p.163. Unlike Adorno, I have stressed Cabeza de Vaca's strategic *Silences*.

49 to Cipangu. See the description of Antillia by William H. Tillinghast in Justin Winsor, *Narrative and Critical History of America*, 8 vols. (Boston, 1889), 1:31–49, and 2:102–4.

49 seven caves. Adolph Francis Bandelier, *Hemenway Southwestern Archaeological Expedition: Contributions to the History of the Southwestern Portion of the United States,* Papers of the Archaeological Institute of America, American Series 5 (Cambridge MA, 1890), pp.5–11. Aztlan was the mythical land of the North from which the Aztecs and related tribes traced their descent.

49 "no metal but gold." From Garcia Ordoñez de Montalvo's continuation of the Amadis of Gaul cycle, *Las Sergas de Esplandian* (1510?), quoted in Winsor, *Narrative and Critical History of America*, 2:443.

49 called them up. See Irving A. Leonard, *Books of the Brave: Being an Account of Books and of Men in the Spanish Conquest and Settlement of the Sixteenth Century New World* (Cambridge MA, 1949), p.13. The initial chapters of John J. O'Connor's *Amadis de Gaule and Its Influence on Elizabethan Literature* (New Brunswick NJ, 1970), give good descriptions of the themes and contents of the romances. It is interesting to note that a royal Spanish decree of 1531 "forbade the importation of chivalric romances into the Spanish colonies of the New World on the ground that the books were idle and profane, and a later edict banned their printing." O'Connor, *Amadis de Gaule*, pp.9–10. Both the decree and the edict were easily evaded.

50 Paladin Roland. Bernal Díaz, *The Conquest of New Spain,*, trans. J. M. Cohen (Harmondsworth, 1963), p.84.

50 not a dream. Díaz, *The Conquest of New Spain*, p.214.

50 cured by gold. Todorov, *The Conquest of America*, p.96.

50 "cannot see them." Richard Hakluyt, *The Principal Navigations, Voyages, Traffiques & Discoveries of the English Nation*, 10 vols. (1598–1600; London, 1927), 6:283.

50 silver workers. George Parker Winship, *The Coronado Expedition, 1540–1542*, Bureau of American Ethnology, vol. 14, part 1, (Washington DC, 1896), pp.472–73.

51 "a great cross." Percy M. Baldwin, "Fray Marcos de Niza and His Discovery of the Seven Cities of Cíbola," *New Mexico Historical Review* 1 (April 1926): 204.

51 Cíbola. The name Cíbola may be from an Opata word meaning *Zuni*. The Spaniards later used the term *cibolo* for the American bison. See Winsor, *Narrative
and Critical History of America*, 2:477, and David J. Weber, *The Spanish Frontier in North America* (New Haven CT, 1992), p.46.

51 rattles and bells. Winship, *The Coronado Expedition*, p.360.

52 black man before them? Winship, *The Coronado Expedition*, pp.360–61, 475
(translation of Castañeda's narrative of the Coronado expedition), Baldwin,
"Fray Marcos de Niza and his Discovery of the Seven Cities of Cibola," pp.214–
15.

52 to the witch. Ruth L. Bunzel, *Introduction to Zuni Ceremonialism*, 47th Annual
Report of the Bureau of American Ethnology, Smithsonian Institute (Washington DC, 1929–30), p.479.

52 and iron forges. Winship, *The Coronado Expedition*, pp.365–66.

52 wished to go. Winship, *The Coronado Expedition*, p.364.

52 "all up together." Winship, translating Castañeda, *The Coronado Expedition*,
p.483.

52 Coronado defeated the Indians. Weber, *The Spanish Frontier in North America*,
pp.15, 22, 367–68.

53 believed the Turk. Winship, translating Castañeda, *The Coronado Expedition*,
p.493.

54 in a fortnight. Winship, translating Castañeda, *The Coronado Expedition*,
pp.508–9.

54 in the fastness of America. Winship, translating Jaramillo, *The Coronado Expedition*, p.590. See also Herbert E. Bolton, *Coronado: Knight of Pueblos and
Plains* (New York, 1949), pp.289–90.

54 would be helpless. George P. Hammond and Agapito Rey, translating Coronado's Letter to the King of 20 October 1541, *Narratives of the Coronado Expedition 1540–1542* (Albuquerque, 1940), pp.187–89. Winship, translating Castañeda, *The Coronado Expedition*, p.509.

54 "came to this place." A. F. Bandelier, *The Gilded Man (El Dorado) and Other
Pictures of the Spanish Occupancy of America* (1893; Chicago, 1962), pp.237,
244.

55 singing in unison. Winship, *The Coronado Expedition*, p.522.

55 "desire to do." Bernal Díaz, quoted in Weber, *The Spanish Frontier in North
America*, p.23.

55 to be deplored. Bunzel, *Introduction to Zuni Ceremonialism*, p.480. The somewhat romantic view of Zuni society found in some of the earlier students of the
pueblos, most eloquently expressed in Ruth Benedict's *Patterns of Culture* (Bos-

ton, 1934), has been modified by subsequent research, which has seen in the obsessive ritualization of life, and pervasive concern about witchcraft, expressions of suppressed aggression. The social organization of pueblo life has similarly been seen as a complex web of negotiations concerning status and gender. A good summary of this new view of aboriginal pueblo social organization may be found in Ramon A. Guitierrez, *When Jesus Came, the Corn Mothers Went Away: Marriage, Sexuality, and Power in New Mexico, 1500–1846* (Stanford CA, 1991).

55 "an opportunity." Winship, translating Castañeda, *The Coronado Expedition,* p.472.

56 "saluting me." "Prayer of Columbus," 1874, 1881. Walt Whitman, *Complete Poetry and Collected Prose,* ed. Justin Kaplan (New York, 1982), p.542.

56 "the grocery boys." Allen Ginsberg, "A Supermarket in California," *Howl and Other Poems* (San Francisco, 1956).

57 "(yet unfound?)" "Facing West from California's Shores," 1860, 1867. Whitman, *Complete Poetry and Collected Prose,* p.267.

CHAPTER THREE: DREAM MINING

60 35,000 people. The estimate is that of Mine believer and historian Norman C. Pierce.

62 "Gospel is true?" Norman C. Pierce, *The Dream Mine Story* (Salt Lake City? 1958; revised 1972), p.2.

63 a vanished people. Pierce, *The Dream Mine Story,* pp.6, 8.

63 was high noon. Pierce, *The Dream Mine Story,* p.13.

64 "warning for me." Pierce, *The Dream Mine Story,* p.13.

64 for $1.50 each. Pierce, *The Dream Mine Story,* p.14.

64 his own mine vision. Wayland D. Hand, "Folklore from Utah's Silver Mining Camps," *Journal of American Folklore* 54 (1941), collected in John Greenway, ed., *Folklore of the Great West* (Palo Alto CA, 1969), pp.291–92. The dates are interesting. Koyle's dream could hardly have influenced Jesse Knight since Koyle kept his dream to himself for so many years. But did Knight's dream and its success influence Koyle and contribute to a retrospective revision of the date of Koyle's first dream of the mountain? Hand suggests that Knight's munificence toward the Mormon Church during one of its financial crises may have influenced Koyle's ultimate vision of his mine as a "City of Refuge." Hand lists other Utah Dream Mines; see Hand's article in Greenway's *Folklore of the Great West,* p.292.

64 about the Mine. See also Mormon 2:10 and Helaman 13:31 and 35–38.

64 a boarding house? See Doctrine and Covenants 124:22–24 and 56–82. A sample: "Verily I say unto you, let my servant Joseph pay stock into their hands for the building of that house, as seemeth him good; but my servant Joseph cannot pay over fifteen thousand dollars stock in that house, nor under fifty dollars; neither can any other man, saith the Lord." Doctrine and Covenants 124:72.

65 theological enterprise. Pierce, *The Dream Mine Story*, pp.20–22. According to Joseph Smith a portion of the Book of Mormon was similarly "sealed."

65 shut for six years. Pierce, *The Dream Mine Story*, pp.57, 30.

65 Church Co-Operative. Pierce, *The Dream Mine Story*, pp.30, 31.

66 said as Apostle. Pierce, *The Dream Mine Story*, p.38.

66 the entire property. Pack's article is reproduced in Pierce, *The Dream Mine Story*, p.41.

66 stockholders were satisfied. Pierce, *The Dream Mine Story*, pp.42, 44.

67 at the mill house. Pierce, *The Dream Mine Story*, pp.14, 71–73, 77–78.

67 "Year of Prosperity." Pierce, *The Dream Mine Story*, pp.47–48, 83.

67 he wept. Raymond Taylor to Samuel Taylor, 10 January 1947, John Taylor Family Papers, MS 50, BX 57, Fd. 2, Marriott Library, Special Collections, University of Utah, Salt Lake City.

67 in the *Deseret News*. Salt Lake City *Deseret News*, 8 January 1947.

68 "legal right now." Raymond Taylor to Samuel Taylor, 18 April 1948. John Taylor Family Papers, MS 50, BX 57, Fd. 3.

68 as he wished. Pierce, *The Dream Mine Story*, pp.91–96, 98.

68 "vanished away." Pierce, *The Dream Mine Story*, pp.61–62.

69 the financial crash. Pierce, *The Dream Mine Story*, pp.54–56.

69 "of this great work." Pierce, *The Dream Mine Story*, p.80.

70 Mormon fundamentalists. Lee Nelson, "Dream Mine: Utah's Century-Old Treasure Hunt," *Utah Holiday*, November 1985, pp.36–45.

71 "none for you!" Pierce, *The Dream Mine Story*, p.142.

CHAPTER FOUR: COWBOYS, WOBBLIES, AND
THE MYTH OF THE WEST

73 into its final form. Owen Wister, *The Virginian: A Horseman of the Plains* (New York, 1902).

74 Arizona Territory. Chester A. Arthur, "First Annual Message to the Senate and House of Representatives of the United States," 6 December 1881. Reprinted in

Frank Bergon and Zeese Papanikolas, eds., *Looking Far West: The Search for the American West in History, Myth and Literature* (New York, 1978), pp.273–74.

74 "self-confidence." Theodore Roosevelt, *Ranch Life and the Hunting-Trail* (New York, 1888), p.9.

74 Wister, had it. Owen Wister, "The Evolution of the Cow-Puncher," *Harper's New Monthly Magazine* 91 (September 1895), reprinted in Ben Merchant Vorpahl, ed., *My Dear Wister—The Frederic Remington-Owen Wister Letters* (Palo Alto CA, 1972), pp.77–96.

75 (Wyoming's Sweetwater?) Edward Aveling and Eleanor Marx Aveling, *The Working-Class Movement in America* (London, 1891), p.156. For accounts of the Wyoming and other cowboy strikes see David E. Lopez, "Cowboy Strikes and Unions," *Labor History* 18 (summer 1977): 325–40; and David Dary, *Cowboy Culture* (1981; New York, 1982), pp.302–7.

75 "may grow himself." Aveling and Aveling, *The Working-Class Movement*, pp.154–65 (emphasis in original).

75 "yappy, yay!" Jay Monaghan, *Schoolboy, Cowboy, Mexican Spy* (Berkeley CA, 1977), p.53.

76 and rode away. Charles A. Siringo, *A Texas Cowboy, or Fifteen Years on the Hurricane Deck of a Spanish Pony* (1885; Lincoln NE, 1966), pp. xv–xvi, 52.

76 "natural." Roland Barthes, *Mythologies*, trans. Annette Lavers (New York, 1975), p.143.

76 ten years past. For the involvement of Wister's rancher friends in the Johnson County War, see G. Edward White, *The Eastern Establishment and the Western Experience* (New Haven CT, 1968), pp.127–29.

77 "new gradin'." Owen Wister, *The Virginian* (1902; New York, 1928), p.141.

78 "was a soldier." Frederic Remington, "Chicago under the Mob," *Harper's Weekly,* 21 July 1894, reprinted in *The Collected Writings of Frederic Remington,* ed. Peggy Samuels and Harold Samuels (New York, 1979), pp.152–54. Quotation p.153.

78 "to the top." Remington, "Chicago under the Mob," p.154.

78 the Western myth. "There is a big foreign population here in Chicago, which isn't American in any particular, and it follows readily any demagogue with revolutionary tendencies. . . . Eventually this unlicked mob will have to be shot up a little, or washed, before it will get into a mental calm." Remington, "Chicago under the Law," *Harper's Weekly* 28 July 1894, reprinted in Samuels and Samuels, *The Collected Writings of Frederic Remington,* pp.156–57. See also Richard Maxwell Brown, "Western Violence: Structure, Values, Myth," *Western Historical Quarterly* 24 (February 1933): 5–20. Brown sees such violent events

as the Johnson County War and the Tonto Basin War of 1887–88 as part of a "Western Civil War of Incorporation" promulgated by the "conservative, consolidating authority of modern capitalistic forces" (p.6). By 1919 the myth of the West was ready to take on the Wobblies, who represented the very essence of all the capitalists abhorred. Zane Grey's wartime *The Desert of Wheat* (New York, 1919) shows the Wobblies as vicious albeit unwitting tools of German Imperial agents, burning wheat fields and sabotaging equipment with a lurid zest. The answer to this menace lies in the one instance of group solidarity the mythological west seemed to approve of – the Vigilantes. The Wobbly wartime sabotage existed only in Grey's dubious imagination; but the book's mass deportations and summary hanging of an organizer were, unfortunately, based on real events in Bisbee, Arizona, and Butte, Montana. By the novel's end Grey has something of a change of heart toward the Wobblies, seeing them as essentially decent, if deluded workers, who only need to be wooed away from socialism and anarchism by a bigger slice of the economic pie.

79 "and must eat." The account of this trip is taken from Ed Nolan's articles in *The Industrial Worker*, 17, 24 April 1913, reprinted in Philip S. Foner, ed., *Fellow Workers and Friends: I.W.W. Free-Speech Fights as Told by Participants* (Westport CT, 1981), pp.146–52.

80 "Solidarity." Foner, ed., *Fellow Workers and Friends*, pp.149–50.

80 Wobbly train, See James H. Walsh's account of the trip of the "Overall Brigade" from Portland to the I.W.W. convention in Chicago in 1908. *Industrial Union Bulletin*, 19 September 1908, reprinted in Joyce L. Kornbluh, *Rebel Voices* (Ann Arbor MI, 1964), p.42. See also E. M. Clyde on a Wobbly train to the Fresno Free Speech Fight, reprinted in Foner, ed., *Fellow Workers and Friends*, pp.81–82.

81 "got any money?" George Milburn, *The Hobo's Hornbook* (New York, 1930), pp.225–26.

81 vagrancy charge. For a vivid account of the lives of such men see Gregory R. Woirol, *In the Floating Army: F. C. Mills on Itinerant Life in California, 1914* (Urbana IL, 1992).

81 "the men are not." Anne Martin, "Nevada: Beautiful Desert of Buried Hopes," *Nation*, 26 July 1922, pp.89–92.

81 "dirty plates." James A. Young and B. Abbott Sparks, *Cattle in the Cold Desert* (Logan UT, 1985), p.162.

82 "superfluous human being." Walter A. Wyckoff, *The Workers, an Experiment in Reality: The West* (New York, 1898), pp.1–2.

82 "thronging crowd." Wyckoff, *The Workers*, p.63.

82 "human sympathy." Wyckoff, *The Workers*, p.78.

83 "hands of God." Milburn, *The Hobo's Hornbook,* p.251.

83 just the point. See Melvyn Dubofsky, *We Shall Be All: A History of the Industrial Workers of the World* (1969; Urbana IL, 1988), pp.136–41.

84 "worker in the East." *Solidarity,* 21 November 1914. Reprinted in Kornbluh, *Rebel Voices,* pp.66–67.

84 "revive us again." Milburn, *The Hobo's Hornbook,* pp.97–101. See John Greenway, *American Folksongs of Protest* (1953; New York, 1960), pp.197–202, for Wobbly Harry McClintock's claim to composing this song.

85 "bum on the plush." The phrase refers to the capitalist riding in comfort inside the train. Milburn, *The Hobo's Hornbook,* quoted in Kornbluh, *Rebel Voices,* p.77.

85 "to suit ourselves." Kornbluh, *Rebel Voices,* p.50.

85 *their consciousness.* Karl Marx, *A Contribution to the Critique of Political Economy* (1859), translated from the second German edition by N. I. Stone (Chicago, 1904), pp.11–12. Emphasis added.

85 "own environment." *Evidence and Cross-Examination of J. T. (Red) Doran in the Case of U.S.A. vs. Wm. D. Haywood et al.,* reprinted by the General Defense Committee (Chicago, n.d.), p.12. Compare Doran's words to those of Wobbly organizer James P. Thompson: "We say that in order to understand the social problem it must be looked at as a process of natural history, governed not only by laws independent of human will, consciousness and intelligence, but, on the contrary, determining that very will, consciousness, and intelligence." *Final Report and Testimony Submitted to Congress by the United States Commission on Industrial Relations, created by the Act of August 23, 1912* (Washington DC, 1916), 5:4236.

86 kind of rite. See Jerilyn S. McIntyre, *Rituals of Disorder: A Dramatistic Interpretation of Radical Dissent,* Journalism Monographs, no. 112 (Columbia SC, May 1989). Using categories and a methodology drawn from Mikhail Bakhtin and Victor Turner, McIntyre parallels some of the themes of this chapter.

86 "talk long anyhow!" Foner, ed., *Fellow Workers and Friends,* pp.26, 128.

86 in the process. Dubofsky, *We Shall Be All,* pp.196–97.

87 philosophical one. See Kornbluh, *Rebel Voices,* pp.37–38; Dubofsky, *We Shall Be All,* pp.162–64. Salvatore Salerno, *Red November, Black November: Culture and Community in the Industrial Workers of the World* (Albany NY, 1989), p.107, and Fred W. Thompson and Patrick Murfin, *The I.W.W.: Its First Seventy Years: 1905–1975* (Oakland CA, 1976), pp.80–87, also take up the issue of I.W.W. sabotage.

87 "get theirs in." William D. Haywood, *The General Strike* (Chicago, n.d.), reprinted in Kornbluh, *Rebel Voices*, pp.45–51.

88 "dying in peace." William D. Haywood, testimony in *Final Report and Testimony Submitted to Congress by the United States Commission on Industrial Relations*, 11:10574, 10579.

88 Strike is myth. Georges Sorel saw the myth of the General Strike in somewhat different terms in 1906 and earlier. For him it is not a utopia, which was always an intellectual product, but a projection into the future of an all-mastering idea, a social myth that is the "expression of a determination to act." Even the failure of such a myth does not devalue it; on the contrary, it merely means the preparation for action has been insufficient, and failure itself is a school creating the true revolutionary. Georges Sorel, *Reflections on Violence*, trans. T. E. Hulme (1906; New York, 1914).

88 "obliteration of time." Claude Lévi-Strauss, *The Raw and the Cooked*, trans. John Weightman and Doreen Weightman (1964; New York, 1970), pp.15–16.

89 in effigy, Roosevelt, *Ranch Life and the Hunting-Trail*, p.109.

89 Pinkerton detective. Charles A. Siringo, *A Cowboy Detective: A True Story of Twenty-Two Years with a World-Famous Detective Agency* (1912; Lincoln NE, 1988), pp.11–23.

89 had ever known. William D. Haywood, *Bill Haywood's Book: The Autobiography of William D. Haywood* (New York, 1929), p.31.

90 would organize. For Siringo's dubious role in the Coeur D'Alene troubles of 1892 see Dubovsky, *We Shall Be All*, pp.30–32.

90 strike of 1883. This is an inference. In *Riata and Spurs* (Boston, 1927), his last book, Siringo devotes a couple of pages to the strike, which he claims was put down by his friend Pat Garrett at the head of a force of Texas Rangers. Siringo does not mention his own participation, and his memoirs for those years give us a seamless succession of roundups and errands for his beloved boss D. T. Beals, a wealthy Boston manufacturer. See Lopez, "Cowboy Strikes and Unions," pp.330–33.

90 trial for his life. Siringo claims to have warned officials of a plot to lynch Haywood and his fellow defendants after the trial. See Ben E. Pingenot, *Siringo* (College Station TX, 1989), p.63.

90 the movie screen. Pingenot, *Siringo*, pp.100–110.

CHAPTER FIVE: THE ROAD TO OZ

92 "*Providence.*" Lansford W. Hastings, *The Emigrants' Guide to Oregon and California* (Cincinnati, 1845), pp.151–52.

93 "open crowds." The terminology is Elias Canetti's. See Elias Canetti, *Crowds and Power,* trans. Carol Stewart (1960; New York, 1978), pp.16–17.

93 farm in Anaheim. See Robert V. Hine, *California's Utopian Colonies* (1953; New York, 1973).

94 "stamps and parchment." Thomas Bullock, letter in the *Latter-Day Saints' Millennial Star* [Liverpool] (15 April 1848): 117–18.

94 "always landing." Oscar Wilde, *The Soul of Man under Socialism* (1891) in *The Annotated Oscar Wilde,* ed. H. Montgomery Hyde (New York, 1982), p.406.

95 "the Other Party." Willa Cather, "El Dorado: A Kansas Recessional," *New England Magazine* 24 (June 1901): 364.

95 like an angel. The description of Barnum's museum is from Neil Harris, *Humbug: The Art of P. T. Barnum* (Boston, 1973), pp.165–66; and Constance Rourke, *Trumpets of Jubilee* (New York, 1927), pp.395–96.

96 (Shakespeare's cottage). P. T. Barnum, *Struggles and Triumphs,* ed. Carl Bode (1869; New York, 1981), p.221.

96 (juveniles?). Phineas T. Barnum, *Struggles and Triumphs; or, Forty Years' Recollections of P. T. Barnum Written by Himself* (1869; Hartford CT, 1873), pp.148–51.

96 flatters it. Rourke, *Trumpets of Jubilee,* p.384.

97 "was the public." Rourke, *Trumpets of Jubilee,* p.371.

97 "halls of humbug." So called by Henry James, who visited them as a child. Henry James, *A Small Boy and Others* (New York, 1913), p.155.

98 in their union. Henry Nash Smith, *Virgin Land: The American West as Symbol and Myth* (Cambridge MA, 1950).

98 American Revolution. Interestingly, it is to the Indians, still possessing a large measure of the good utopian virtues, that Crèvecoeur's farmer thinks of fleeing with the coming of war, in *Letters.*

99 muddy streams. For a description of conditions on the Great Plains farmlands in the early days of white settlement see Everett Dick, *The Sod-House Frontier 1854–1890* (New York, 1937), pp.202–31.

99 "everything else." L. Frank Baum, *The Wonderful Wizard of Oz* (1900; New York, 1960), p.12.

99 "to laugh at." Baum, *The Wonderful Wizard of Oz,* pp.12–13.

101 "become nothing." Ignatius Donnelly, *Caesar's Column: A Study of the Twentieth Century* (1890; Cambridge MA, 1960), p.18.

101 "was the air." Donnelly, *Caesar's Column,* p.38.

102 "Q.E.D." Duchamp's note is reproduced in *Salt Seller: The Writings of Marcel*

Duchamp (Marchand du Sel), ed. Michel Sanouillet and Elmer Peterson (New York, 1973), p.74.

103 *Dry Goods Windows*. Quoted in Stuart Culver, "What Manikins Want: *The Wonderful Wizard of Oz* and *The Art of Decorating Dry Goods Windows*," *Representations* 21 (winter 1988): 106.

103 "could not afford." Edward Bellamy, *Looking Backward* (1888; Cleveland, 1946), p.302.

103 "to follow." Bellamy, *Looking Backward*, p.257.

104 wood shavings. Nancy Tystad Koupal, "From the Land of Oz: L. Frank Baum's Satirical View of South Dakota's First Year of Statehood," *Montana: The Magazine of Western History* 40, (spring 1990): 55. Culver, in "What Manikins Want," pp.102–3, discusses the origins of this joke.

104 green lemonade. See Culver, "What Manikins Want," p.103, for a subtler reading of the function of the spectacles: "Popcorn and lemonade are not naturally green, and the citizens are not mistaking the greenness around them for the outward sign of an intrinsic value. Green is not for them the color of food; rather it is the color of gems. . . . Thus consumption, under the influence of the green spectacles, becomes an endless cycle of visual fascinations and mistaken appropriations; desiring green, the Ozites pursue value in the abstract, which is manifest only in the moment before one consumes a thing or puts it to use."

105 "die unnoticed." Quoted by S. J. Sackett, "The Utopia of Oz," collected in L. Frank Baum, *The Wizard of Oz*, ed. Michael Patrick Hearn (New York, 1983), p.215.

105 already have. Culver, in "What Manikins Want," points out that the three petitioners already know the Wizard is a fraud when they accept the symbolic brains, heart, and courage from him.

105 "I must admit." Baum, *The Wonderful Wizard of Oz*, p.189.

105 "can't be done?" Baum, *The Wonderful Wizard of Oz*, p.199.

106 suffragettes. For descriptions of the utopian concepts of the later Oz books, see Edward Wagenknecht, "Utopia Americana," and Sackett, "The Utopia of Oz," collected in Baum, *The Wizard of Oz*, ed. Hearn.

107 "own heart." Alexis de Tocqueville, *Democracy in America*, 2 vols., trans. Phillips Bradley (New York, 1945), 2:99.

CHAPTER SIX: MX

111 "Sinews of Peace." Winston S. Churchill, *The Sinews of Peace: Post-War Speeches by Winston S. Churchill*, ed. Randolph S. Churchill (Boston, 1949), pp.93–105.

114 Emperor's palace. An excellent synopsis of the psychology of nuclear America since the 1950s can be found in the epilogue of Paul Boyer's *By the Bomb's Early Light* (New York, 1985).

114 tensions of the Cold War. For a chilling example of such scenarios see Herman Kahn, *On Escalation: Metaphors and Scenarios* (Hudson Institute, 1965), pp.34–43.

114 mutual destruction. Thomas C. Schelling, "What Went Wrong with Arms Control?" *Foreign Affairs* 64 (winter 1985–86): 230.

114 an addiction. E. P. Thompson, *Beyond the Cold War: A New Approach to the Arms Race and Nuclear Annihilation* (New York, 1982), pp.1–24.

116 impose limitations. Albert Einstein once gave a succinct statement of what he thought of such arms limitations treaties. He asked us to consider a city whose citizens were noted for mayhem and violence. Imagine, he said, the idea of laws for such a city that did not ban knives, but simply regulated the length of their blades.

116 no real military purpose; Schelling, "What Went Wrong with Arms Control?" p.228. Good general accounts of the MX system and its history can be found in John Edwards, *Superweapon: The Making of MX* (New York, 1982) and Herbert Scoville Jr., *MX: Prescription for Disaster* (Cambridge MA, 1981).

116 must be hidden. That we already had such concealable mobile missile systems, in our fleet of submarine-launched Polaris missiles, was not a strong enough argument for those who continued to uphold the orthodoxy that our missile defense system must be three-legged: based on invulnerable systems on land, air, and sea.

117 the Great Basin. Early on the Texas Panhandle was also considered as a base for the mobile system, and a draft environmental impact statement was prepared. How seriously the Panhandle was considered is questionable. I find it likely it was simply thrown in as a token to mollify Great Basin congressional leaders and their constituents.

117 dollars attached to it. The Carter administration's initial estimate was $33.2 billion. Costs of more than $100 billion were estimated by other agencies, not counting the $425 million or so it would cost annually to operate the system.

118 for three years. Seattle *Post-Intelligencer,* 3 May 1981, as cited in Julie Anne Stephens, "Socio-Economic Impacts of the MX Missile Project: A Case Study of Caliente, Nevada," senior thesis, Departments of Geography and Anthropology, Vassar College, 1982, p.66.

119 twenty to thirty years. Erica Shoenberger, "Selling the MX," *Progressive* 44 (May 1980): 16, as cited in Stephens, "Case Study of Caliente, Nevada," p.72.

119 "by 1989." Dr. William J. Perry, quoted in Scott M. Matheson with James Edwin Kee, *Out of Balance* (Salt Lake City, 1986), p.59.

120 "devils worshipped." Michael Wigglesworth in 1662, quoted in Henry Nash Smith, *Virgin Land: The American West as Symbol and Myth* (1950; Cambridge MA, 1970), p.4.

120 Utah-Nevada border. Matheson and Key, *Out of Balance*, p.61.

121 on Eastern money. Compare Donald Worster on the West's dependence on the military in *Under Western Skies: Nature and History in the American West* (New York, 1992), p.11: "How could one, for example, write about World War II's impact and leave out the glaring fact that this region henceforth would be dominated by the military-industrial complex, that its economic health would rise and fall with the prospects of the Pentagon and the Cold War, a fact that is obvious today from San Diego's navy yards all the way to Montana's missile silos? Or how could one leave off that list of so-called achievements the doomsday shadow of the atomic bomb – the fact that the West has been forever poisoned by nuclear fallout and, since the war, has found itself sick and dying of radiation, beset by the problems of nuclear waste disposal, living in white-knuckled fear in the vicinity of such places as Rocky Flats Arsenal, Alamogordo, Los Alamos, Hanford, and the Nevada test site?"

122 "for the future." Edward Abbey, *Down the River* (New York, 1982), p.85.

123 have on their lives. Information on Caliente and the MX is from Stephens, "Case Study of Caliente, Nevada. . ."

125 "have brought here." Quotations from the participants in the Cedar City meeting and from the Indians at Battle Mountain are from National Public Radio's audio tape *The MX Missile Reports,* NPR, Washington DC, 1981.

125 on human beings. Matheson and Key, *Out of Balance*, p.82.

125 "Business Opportunity Newsletter." Stephens, "Case Study of Caliente, Nevada," pp.74–75.

125 check out each other's action. Scoville, MX: *Prescription for Disaster,* p.190.

126 won back the dead. Robert H. Lowie, "Shoshonean Tales," *Journal of American Folk-Lore* 37 (January–June 1924): 229–31.

127 "may be short." Churchill, *The Sinews of Peace,* p.99.

127 "its implications." Henry A. Kissinger, *Years of Upheaval,* cited in Robert Jay Lifton and Richard Falk, *Indefensible Weapons: The Political and Psychological Case against Nuclearism* (New York, 1982), p.134.

127 outthink him. This is the "useful" enemy of Richard Falk's trenchant phrase, allowing the construction of "an essential identity" around the imagery of the hated opponent. Lifton and Falk, *Indefensible Weapons,* p.209.

127 to predict. See Alvin M. Saperstein, "Chaos – A Model for the Outbreak of War," *Nature*, 24 May 1984, pp.303–5.

128 "sakiz." Oakland *Tribune*, 15 September 1985.

128 its own solution. See Thomas C. Schelling's study of military gamesmanship in the Nuclear Age, *The Strategy of Conflict* (1960; Cambridge MA, 1980), pp.279–80: "Both players, in effect, accept a common authority – the power of the game to dictate its own solution through their intellectual capacity to perceive it – and what they expect is that they both perceive the same solution."

129 might mean jobs. Salt Lake *Tribune*, 14 August 1980.

129 "of civilization." Quoted in Matheson and Key, *Out of Balance*, p.84.

CHAPTER SEVEN: NEWS FROM NOWHERE

133 "for a storm." Edmund Wilson, *The Thirties* (1980; New York, 1982), p.115.

133 lawns at night. Castle's story is told in his letter to a Los Angeles attorney published in the *Nation*. Victor Castle, "Well, I Quit My Job at the Dam," *Nation* 133 (26 August 1931): 207–8.

134 second-degree burns. Laton McCartney, *Friends in High Places: The Bechtel Story, the Most Secret Corporation and How It Engineered the World* (New York, 1988), p.35.

134 heads in Las Vegas. For a description of Boulder City see Joseph E. Stevens, *Hoover Dam: An American Adventure* (Norman OK, 1988), pp.117–58.

134 brave illusions. The I.W.W. organization drive fizzled at Hoover Dam, but the literature of their failed attempt shows them still possessing the *brio* of their earlier days and still capable of writing devastating poems and parodies. See Stevens, *Hoover Dam*, pp.65–79, 204–6, 235–36, 278–80, 282; Edmund Wilson, *The American Earthquake* (Garden City NY, 1958), pp.368–77; and Guy Louis Rocha, "The IWW and the Boulder Canyon Project: The Final Death Throes of American Syndicalism," *Nevada Historical Quarterly* 21 (spring 1978): 3–24.

134 buried in the dam. Stevens, *Hoover Dam*, pp.219–21.

135 foundations of the dam. See Donald Worster, *Under Western Skies: Nature and History in the American West* (New York, 1992), pp.77–78. "Even at this very moment the Colorado River is busy preparing to saw through the Hoover Dam, laying down its silt behind the wall, gathering force to remove this new obstruction just as it has removed everything else ever put in its way by the forces of geology."

135 The Philosopher. Sometime in the mid-1980s the philosopher Jean Baudrillard traveled to the United States and left notes on his journey in the form of a book.

No one but Baudrillard himself knows precisely where he went during that trip, what he saw or what he did. In order to supplement that work I have imagined another philosopher taking a similar trip who happens to think some of the same thoughts. See, by way of comparison, Jean Baudrillard, *America*, trans. Chris Turner (1986; London, 1988).

135 century longest. William H. Gass, *The World within the Word* (New York, 1978), p.65.

135 for the future. Baudrillard, *America*.

136 the daylight. Robert Venturi, Denise Scott Brown, and Steven Izenour, *Learning from Las Vegas: The Forgotten Symbolism of Architectural Form* (1977; Cambridge MA, 1991), pp.8–18.

139 history, class. Morris Lapidus, architect of Miami's Hotel Fontainebleau: "People are looking for illusions; they don't want the world's realities. And, I asked, where do I find this world of illusion? Where are their tastes formulated? Do they study it in school? Do they go to museums? Do they travel in Europe? Only one place – the movies. They go to the movies. The hell with everything else." Quoted in Venturi, Brown, and Izenour, *Learning from Las Vegas*, p.80.

139 "constraining order." Venturi, Brown, and Izenour, *Learning from Las Vegas*, p.77.

141 "isn't it?" A. Alvarez, *The Biggest Game in Town* (Boston, 1983), p.123.

143 book on Las Vegas. Mario Puzo, *Inside Las Vegas* (New York, 1977), p.209.

144 "the local highway." Venturi, Brown, and Izenour, *Learning from Las Vegas*, p.35.

144 "of the water." Francis H. Leavitt, "The Influence of the Mormon People in the Settlement of Clark County," thesis, University of Nevada, Reno, 1934, p.43.

144 the corn grow. Material on the Mormon colony in Las Vegas is drawn from Leavitt, "The Influence of the Mormon People in the Settlement of Clark County"; Stanley W. Paher, *Las Vegas as It Began, as It Grew* (Las Vegas, 1971), pp.19–31; Leonard J. Arrington, *The Mormons in Nevada* (Las Vegas, 1979), pp.22–25; and Eugene E. Campbell, "Brigham Young's Outer Cordon – A Reappraisal," *Utah Historical Quarterly* 41 (summer 1973): 231–35.

145 "how much." Paher, *Las Vegas as It Began, as It Grew,* p.31.

145 anymore in Las Vegas? Isabel T. Kelly, "Southern Paiute Shamanism," *Anthropological Records* 2 (November 1939): 164.

APPENDIX: SHOSHONE MYTHS AND THEIR RETELLING

155 "with wild delight." John Wesley Powell, *Anthropology of the Numa: John Wesley Powell's Manuscripts on the Numic Peoples of Western North America,*

1868–1880, ed. Don D. Fowler and Catherine S. Fowler, *Smithsonian Contributions to Anthropology* 14 (Washington DC, 1971), p.73.

156 "each other stories." The translation of the term comes from Sven Liljeblad's exemplary essay "Oral Tradition: Content and Style of Verbal Arts," *Handbook of North American Indians,* 11:650.

156 the supernatural. Liljeblad, "Oral Tradition," 11:641.

156 we now inhabit. Powell reproduces a southern Paiute version of the Origin of People story and comments that this account conflicts with their general belief that they and the other tribes descended from the ancients, "but it is a curious fact that they discover no inconsistency, and the glaring contradictions are entirely unnoticed. Any hint that these stories do not agree causes great offense." Powell, *Anthropology of the Numa,* p.78. See also Anna Premo's memory, as reported in Anne M. Smith, *Shoshone Tales* (Salt Lake City, 1993), p.79: "Sometimes when two or three old men are telling a tale, they can't agree and will argue over the right way to tell it. They also often argue about which moon it is."

Index